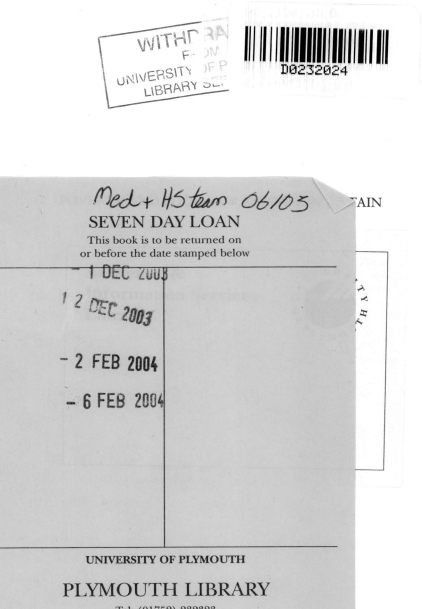

Poverty and Poor Law Reform in Britain: From Chadwick to Booth, 1834–1914

DAVID ENGLANDER

LONGMAN
LONDON AND NEW YORK

Addison Wesley Longman Limited
Edinburgh Gate
Harlow
Essex CM20 2JE
United Kingdom
and Associated Companies throughout the world.

Published in the United States of America
by Addison Wesley Longman, New York

First published 1998

ISBN 0-582 31554 9

British Library Cataloguing-in-Publication Data
A catalogue record for this book is available from the British Library

Library of Congress Cataloging-in-Publication Data

Englander, David, 1949–
Poverty and poor law reform in Britain : from Chadwick to Booth,
1834–1914 / David Englander.
    p.   cm. -- (Seminar studies in history)
Includes bibliographical references and index.
ISBN 0-582-31554-9
1. Poor--Great Britain--History. 2. Poor laws--Great Britain- -History. 3.Public
welfare--Great Britain--History. 4. Poverty--Great Britain--History. I. Title. II. Series.
HV245.E54 1998
362.510941--dc21   97-32650
                                                                                                       CIP

Set by 7 in 10/12 Sabon Roman
Produced through Longman Malaysia, TCP

CONTENTS

AN INTRODUCTION TO THE SERIES

Such is the pace of historical enquiry in the modern world that there is an ever-widening gap between the specialist article or monograph, incorporating the results of current research, and general surveys, which inevitably become out of date. *Seminar Studies in History* are designed to bridge this gap. The series was founded by Patrick Richardson in 1966 and his aim was to cover major themes in British, European and World history. Between 1980 and 1996 Roger Lockyer continued his work, before handing the editorship over to Clive Emsley and Gordon Martel. Clive Emsley is Professor of History at the Open University, while Gordon Martel is Professor of International History at the University of Northern British Columbia, Canada and Senior Research Fellow at De Montfort University.

All the books are written by experts in their field who are not only familiar with the latest research but have often contributed to it. They are frequently revised, in order to take account of new information and interpretations. They provide a selection of documents to illustrate major themes and provoke discussion, and also a guide to further reading. The aim of *Seminar Studies* is to clarify complex issues without over-simplifying them, and to stimulate readers into deepening their knowledge and understanding of major themes and topics.

NOTE ON REFERENCING SYSTEM

Readers should note that numbers in square brackets [5] refer them to the corresponding entry in the Bibliography at the end of the book (specific page numbers are given in italics). A number in square brackets preceded by *Doc.* [*Doc.* 5] refers readers to the corresponding item in the Documents section which follows the main text. Words which are defined in the Glossary are asterisked at first occurrence. There is also a guide to Main Characters and these are also asterisked at first occurrence in the text.

PREFACE

Poverty and Poor Law Reform has been fun to write and a rather more pleasurable experience than the subject matter might seem to suggest. Much of it comes from the range, depth, diversity and erudition of the scholarship on which I have drawn. Anyone who enters this field will be amazed, delighted and inspired by the quality and originality of the studies published thus far. It is not, however, the sole source of indebtedness. Colleagues have been no less encouraging. I am grateful to Clive Emsley who first suggested the project and has been supportive throughout. I have benefited from conversations with Tom Caldwell, who knows more about the history of the Royal Statistical Society than anyone has a right to, and from Richard Thompson whose knowledge of poor law history is stupendous. Rosemary O'Day not only read and commented on the typescript of this study, but generously allowed me to consult the manuscript of her forthcoming book, *Katharine Buildings, East Smithfield, 1880–1914*. I have also benefited from the inquisitiveness of our young sons, Daniel and Matthew, to whom this volume is dedicated.

David Englander
Charles Booth Centre
The Open University

PART ONE: THE CONTEXT

1   INTRODUCTION

The Poor Law Amendment Act of 1834 was the single most important piece of social legislation ever enacted. Its radical redefinition of
the principles of social policy fixed the parameters for all subsequent
debate and discussion. Its organizing assumptions cast a continuing
shadow over attitudes towards the nature of social obligation and dependency. Its imagery, stamped so firmly on our collective memory,
invigorates research, sustains controversy and underscores the continuing relevance of historical understanding in our everyday lives. The
Poor Law touched almost every aspect of life and labour in Victorian
Britain. Employment and wages, housing and rents, migration and
settlement, medicine, marriage, charity and education – all were influenced in one way or another. Relations between rich and poor
were shaped by the Poor Law and local party politics energized by
the controversies that surrounded it. Not surprisingly, the New Poor
Law remains difficult to characterize. Was it progressive or reaction-
ary, malevolent or misguided? Opinions differ. For some scholars the
reformed Poor Law represents the triumph of ideology over reality;
for others the victory of common sense over chaos. Poor relief also
raises issues respecting continuity and innovation in social theory and
social practice. How far was the reformed Poor Law an extension of
the unreformed Poor Law and to what extent did it constitute a radical break with the past? Other issues which excite debate include the
transition from pauperism to poverty and the redefinition of the social question in the late-nineteenth century. Of interest, too, is the
significance of the Poor Law for the long-term development of social
policy. Questions also arise concerning the nature of poor law
studies. Is it, in fact, possible to write a satisfactory poor law history?
Must we make do with institutional accounts from which dependency
and the pauper experience are forever excluded by the importance
assigned to the policy-making process? These and related issues are
considered in the account presented below.

There was, of course, no such thing as a British poor law system.

The public organization of relief in Scotland was quite separate from that in force south of the border. Unlike the system in England and Wales, Scottish social administration was based upon the kirk session (i.e., minister and elders) rather than the civil parish and the right to relief was also restricted. Only the 'destitute' and 'disabled' could claim relief; the able-bodied unemployed, for whom the English Poor Law made provision, were excluded. Both systems, though national in coverage, were dissimilar in their funding arrangements. Scottish poor relief included a large voluntary element; whereas the poor law in England and Wales was distinctive in being a universal system of tax-financed relief. The principle of a legal, compulsory, secular national system of relief was established in a series of enactments of the late-sixteenth century that was consolidated in the celebrated statute known as the 43rd Elizabeth of 1601 [31]. The Tudor legislation made it obligatory on the authorities to provide relief and work. It made the parish the basic unit of administration, provided for a compulsory poor rate to be levied on occupiers of land and houses by overseers appointed by local justices and specified various types of relief for various classes of the needy – alms and almshouses for the aged and infirm, apprenticeship for children, work for the able-bodied and punishment for the work-shy. Punitive measures were also directed at those masterless migratory elements who might settle and become a burden to the ratepayers. Concern to prevent strangers from establishing a residence and so qualifying for poor relief prompted the passage of the Act of Settlement of 1662 which provided for the removal of newcomers who, not being property owners or people of means, might become chargeable to the parish [29, 33, 35].

The system that subsequently developed in the fifteen and a half thousand parishes in England and Wales, though extremely varied in its standards and relief practices, consisted of three basic features: the workhouse, outdoor relief and the settlement regulations. The workhouse, conceived by the Tudors as a means of setting the poor to work, supplied the focus of public debate. Much of it was concerned with cost-cutting and coercion, although space was reserved for possible improvements in social assistance. In practice most workhouses served as almshouses. Outdoor relief was both more extensive and more flexible. It embraced payments for all sorts and conditions – weekly pensions to the aged and infirm, payments for the foster care of village orphans and the upkeep of illegitimate children; casual doles for those in need due to unemployment or sickness; payments for doctor's bills and grants of food, fuel and clothing, particularly during periods of dearth. Allowances to raise wages above the level of subsistence were also granted to poor labourers from the mid-eighteenth century onwards. The darker side to the Old Poor Law came in the form of the settlement regulations which, as noted earlier, placed control over the movement of the labouring population into the hands of overseers and magistrates. Labourers who took off in search of work without a settlement certificate were liable to be arrested as vagrants and deported to the parish of their birth. Condemned by Adam Smith* on civil and economic grounds, the settlement laws were an expression of the growing incoherence of the system of poor relief. By the close of the eighteenth century the aims and objects of social administration seemed wanting in clarity and focus. Was unemployment a form of misfeasance or misfortune? Should relief be administered as a deterrent, a dole or a wage payment? To these and cognate questions there was no satisfactory reply [27, 32].

The demand for a centralized and uniform Poor Law arose primarily from the rising cost of relief. Sustained population growth from the mid-eighteenth century onwards coupled with the increasing commercialization of agriculture led to a growing imbalance between rural labourers and rural employment. Deteriorating living standards were aggravated by the laws of settlement which immobilized surplus labourers in their parish. Wages fell but poor rates soared as the local authorities tried to muddle through by means of doles, work-creation schemes and diverse income supplements. It made no difference. Their size and limited resources were unequal to the task even if their capacity to cope was not impaired by jobbery and corruption. Parliament, in search of a solution, appointed a bevy of committees who worried away at the problem without producing the reassurance that was required. Between 1790 and 1820 the poor rate quadrupled. Within the propertied classes there spread a deep sense of unease. The movement from moral economy* to political economy* and from relationships regulated by custom to relationships regulated by cash was unsettling. Not only were costs rising, so were the poor. Laxity and mismanagement in relief practices were held responsible for the immiseration that transformed deferential labourers into saucy paupers with criminal inclinations. By 1830 the poor rate accounted for one-fifth of the national expenditure. Farmers were going under. Captain Swing was abroad. Riots, rick-burnings and machine-breakings were in progress and the comfortable classes disturbed. Something had to be done. Even before the franchise question had been resolved, ministers were preparing for a final engagement with the unreformed Poor Law [28, 30]. Our study begins at this point. It proceeds from an exploration of the attitudes towards the poor as embodied in the writings of economic and social theorists to an account of the policies and practices of the reformed Poor Law. Chapter 2 surveys the development of poor law policy in England and Wales in the three-quarters of a century which separated the Royal Commission of 1905–9 from that of 1832–34. Chapter 3 moves from policy to experience to examine the character of the workhouse regime, the life of the inmates and popular attitudes towards poor relief. Chapter 4 provides a synoptic view of the Poor Law in Scotland to compare and contrast developments in social policy with the system of poor relief in England and Wales. Chapter 5 examines the impact of social investigation upon contemporary understandings of poverty and poor law reform. Chapter 6 is concerned with problems of historical inquiry and the place of the Poor Law in British history.

PART TWO: DESCRIPTIVE ANALYSIS

2 POOR LAW POLICY IN ENGLAND AND WALES

POVERTY AND THE POOR

'Every one but an idiot knows that the lower classes must be kept poor or they will never be industrious' [16a *p. 361*]. Arthur Young's forceful statement, written in 1771, summarized the deeply held pessimism that characterized social theory from the Tudors to the Hanoverians. Idleness and the suppression thereof supplied its principal theme. Allegedly the besetting sin of the labourer, it was castigated by the godly and criticized by the worldly in about equal measure. Idleness linked questions of sloth, depravity and disorder with problems of productivity and power; it imparted a punitive character to social policy and provided the main justification for a low wage economy. To be sure, there were eighteenth-century writers who argued for a rise in living standards as an incentive to greater effort, but the idea that labour consisted of consumers whose satisfaction was the end of the productive process was still in its infancy. Contemporary wisdom held that high wages promoted indolence, riot and dissipation and that only by payment of barely subsistent wages could the poor be compelled into work and submission [39, 40, 41].

Poverty was understood as the normal and irremediable condition of the population. 'Poverty', wrote economist and social reformer Patrick Colquhoun,* 'is that state and condition in society where the individual has no surplus labour in store, or, in other words, no property or means of subsistence but what is derived from the constant exercise of industry in the various occupations of life' [11 *p. 7*]. No sharp distinction separated the 'labourer' from the 'poor'. Indeed, until the eve of the Industrial Revolution the two were practically synonymous. In common parlance the term 'labouring poor' applied to all who were compelled to work for their daily bread. It was also assumed that the earnings of those so classified would be insufficient for maintenance and from time to time require supplementation from private charity or public relief. The 'labouring poor' thus embraced the poor with the pauper, the independent with the dependent poor and the deserving with the undeserving poor. These impoverished myriads, claimed Arthur Young, constituted 90 per cent of the population. Contemporaries, though, were not alarmed. Poverty not only supplied an inducement to labour, it was widely regarded as the necessary and indispensable basis of civilization and prosperity. 'Without a large proportion of poverty', wrote Colquhoun, in 1806, 'there could be no riches, since riches are the offspring of labour, while labour can result only from a state of poverty; ... without poverty there could be no riches, no refinement, no comfort, and no benefit to those who may be possessed of wealth, inasmuch as, without a large proportion of poverty, surplus labour could never be rendered productive in procuring either the convenience or luxuries of life' [11 *pp.* 7–9].

By 1832, the year in which the Royal Commission on the Poor Laws was appointed, thinking about poverty had changed decisively. The all inclusive notion of the 'labouring poor' had been superseded by a new concept of poverty in which dependency and non-dependency were the organizing principles. Debate on the social question henceforth centred on the distinction between the 'pauper' and the 'poor' The redefinition of terms reflected the influence of a new individualist political economy and arose directly from the social dislocation that accompanied the demographic and industrial revolutions and the hardships created by protracted warfare and dearth [124]. In response to this distress the authorities had sanctioned an enormous expansion in the level and forms of public relief. Experiments included relief in money and kind, subsidized public works and indoor relief in the workhouse. Most significant of all such schemes was the Speenhamland or allowance system introduced in 1795. Meeting against a background of bad harvests and high prices the Berkshire magistrates, who assembled at the Pelican Inn in the village of Speenhamland near Newbury, decided to supplement agricultural wages with poor law allowances on a scale that varied in accordance with the price of bread and the size of the labourers' family. The policy of making up wages out of the rates – rates in aid of wages, as it was called – to cope with the social emergency was endorsed by parliament the following year and adopted widely throughout the southern counties thereafter.

The Speenhamland system transformed the character of poor relief. The terms on which relief was given were recast so as to embrace all – employed and unemployed – whose income fell below a minimum subsistence level. The soaring costs of poor relief registered the transformation that had been wrought and prompted a re-examination of the principles of poor law policy. Critics charged that the expansion of poor relief undermined individual initiative, promoted dependency upon the parish and made labourers into paupers. Some fixed upon the adverse effects on the labour market. Relief payments were said to be injurious to the skill, diligence and honesty of the agricultural labourer. Others pointed to depressed wages, reduced productivity and labour immobility. Still others focused upon the premium placed upon immorality by the relief claimed for bastards and bemoaned the blunting of the work ethic among the industrious poor who could secure more from the parish than could be earned in honest labour [42]. A significant intervention came from Edmund Burke (1729–1797). His *Thoughts and Details of Scarcity* (1795), written shortly after the introduction of the Speenhamland system, was a notable attempt to rethink the idea of the labouring poor in order to demarcate, for purposes of relief policy, those who worked for their subsistence from those who could not work and were dependent upon charity or relief. Burke's intention was to introduce a firm line of division between the pauper and non-pauper as the basis for a significant reduction in the scope of social policy. In subsequent writings he protested against the 'political canting language', the 'puling jargon' of the expression 'labouring poor', in favour of a rigorous distinction that excluded the able-bodied from the purview of the Poor Law. The most important contribution to this debate came from the pen of the Revd Thomas Robert Malthus (1766–1834). His pamphlet, *An Essay on the Principle of Population, As It Affects the Future Improvement of Society*, published in 1798, became one of the foundational texts of nineteenth-century social theory [*Doc. 1*]. Whereas previous writers had viewed population growth as a wealth-creating asset, Malthus saw it as a liability, the cause of widespread distress and near permanent poverty. The labouring poor in this vision were pitched into a relentless struggle for existence, a Hobbesian nightmare in which the industrious poor were pulled downwards towards the dependent poor as the latter slipped ever closer towards starvation and death. Progress, the organizing assumption of enlightened thinking, became a distant contingency and perpetual improvement well nigh impossible. Malthus's law of population, which supplied a rationalization for the subsistence theory of wages, was quickly incorporated into the central truths of the new 'dismal science' of political economy.

Malthus proceeded from the assumption that population tends to increase in a geometrical ratio while subsistence can at best be made to increase only in an arithmetical ratio. The tendency of the population to increase faster than the means of subsistence, unless checked by the exercise of prudence and restraint, must be limited by such positive checks as war, famine, disease and misery to keep up the death rate and by preventative checks such as infanticide and abortion to depress the birth rate. Malthus subsequently conceded that, apart from these manifestations of 'misery and vice', population could also be checked through the exercise of moral restraint (i.e., postponement of the age of marriage and strict sexual continence before marriage). Malthus's principle, posited as an inescapable natural law, struck a mortal blow at the visionary ideals of contemporary social reformers who thought that reason, education and goodwill were sufficient to initiate a perfect social order. Poverty had its origins in the unequal race between population and the means of subsistence rather than in the prevailing social and political arrangements. Social breakdown arising from unlimited population growth, he concluded, could only be averted by the individual pursuit of self-interest working within the framework of the institutions of property, marriage and class division.

Malthus's principal fear was that the labourer's 'prudential restraint' and 'love of independence' was being undermined by the provision of poor relief. The subversive influence of the Poor Laws constituted the starting-point of an uncompromising assault on contemporary social policy. Poor law practices, he argued, encouraged improvident marriages and the proliferation of children for whom there was no support with the result that numbers rose, living standards fell and applications for parish relief soared. In that sense, he observed, the Poor Laws served to 'create the poor they maintain'. Apart from the encouragement of carelessness and extravagance, idleness and insobriety, drunkenness and dissipation, the Poor Laws also had the effect of transfering resources from the 'most industrious and worthy' sorts to the lowest classes. The real victims of the Poor Laws, then, were not the recipients of poor relief but the struggling self-supporting elements above them whose position was jeopardized by the libidinous and irresponsible conduct of their fellows. The poor, Malthus insisted, were their own worst enemies 'A labourer who marries without being able to support a family', he wrote, 'may in some respects be considered as an enemy to all his fellow-labourers'. Those who sought to thwart the invariable and inevitable laws of nature by means of public relief were deemed no less culpable. Malthus held that 'dependent poverty ought to be held disgraceful' and the poor laws abolished. In short, the Poor Laws were not so much a solution to the problem of poverty but a large part of the problem itself [44, 45].

THE ROYAL COMMISSION ON THE POOR LAWS, 1832–34

It was the sweep and cogency of Malthus's writing that carried the *Essay on Population* through six editions during the author's lifetime and made its disturbing vision central to the definition and formation of new strategies of relief practice. But it was the rise in the cost of poor relief coupled with rural incendiarism and industrial unrest which at length led to the appointment of a royal commission to inquire into the whole system [110]. Its report, issued in 1834, became a best-seller and the basis of the New Poor Law [7]. The nine-man all-party commission included the bishops of London and Chester and other authorities on the Poor Law. Particularly noteworthy was the appointment of several country gentlemen who were not doctrinaire Benthamites* but had reached convergent conclusions on the basis of their earlier participation in local reform initiatives. Exponents of a 'practical political economy', these men gave voice to the new commercialism that had become rampant in certain parts of the countryside, a new spirit characterized by a movement away from the protection of the poor to the protection of property [140]. Most prominent among the commissioners was the chairman and economist, Nassau Senior (1790–1864), who wrote the analytical portions of the report and Edwin Chadwick* who drafted its final recommendations. Both were lawyers by training and both were disciples of Jeremy Bentham. Chadwick, Bentham's former secretary, owed his position to Senior, who had recommended his appointment.

Edwin Chadwick was one of the most energetic and innovative of public servants. He was a moving force in the factory, Poor Law and sanitary reform movements and a major influence upon the shaping of Victorian social legislation. His credentials in respect of methods of social investigation were no less impressive. A Benthamite from finger to toe, he was driven by a hatred of waste and inefficiency rather than by any personal identification with individual and collective suffering. Chadwick was a bureaucrat rather than a democrat who preferred government by experts and professionals with public action based on empirical inquiry and large-scale administrative reform [115]. He also had an abrasive personality that set him apart from his patron, the more companionable Nassau Senior. The son of wealthy Sephardi* Jews who had converted to Anglicanism, Senior was educated at Eton and Oxford He qualified as a barrister, supported the Whigs and served as professor of political economy at Oxford. An able exponent of classical economics, who was noted for the clarity and precision of his writings, Senior also possessed the social skills in which Chadwick was so singularly deficient [46].

As might be expected of a follower of Bentham, Chadwick had no time for those like Malthus who would abolish the Poor Laws and leave the poor to shift for themselves. To do so implied a denial of bureaucracy, loss of control and abandonment of the Benthamite belief in the possibilities of legislation to coerce competing private and public interests so as to secure social harmony and the general well-being (often described as an artificial identification of conflicting interests). As a *laissez-faire* economist, he also believed in the primacy of the free competitive market in the solution of social problems. Besides questions of cost and want of system, poor relief was objectionable because of its adverse effect on the productivity of labour. Modern historians have argued that the subsidization of wages under the Old Poor Law was a rational and humane response to underemployment in a backward agricultural sector of the economy [34, 36, 37, 44, 49]. It now appears admirably suited to the needs of the age. The unreformed Poor Law, it is suggested, was superior to Continental poor relief. Not only was it tax-funded, nationwide in coverage and comprehensive in its benefits, the Old Poor Law also made a significant contribution to national economic development [51]. Chadwick and his contemporaries, however, thought that the Poor Law acted as a disincentive to industry and the improvement of skills, discouraged mobility, depressed wages and so perpetuated the poverty it was meant to alleviate. What, he felt, was required was a system of poor relief organized on rational and scientific principles that removed public agencies from the setting of wages, diminished dependency and forced labourers to compete for a living in the open labour market. Profits, productivity and employment would thereby increase and living standards rise.

Chadwick was among the twenty-six assistant commissioners appointed by the Royal Commission on the Poor Laws to travel the country and gather evidence. He was responsible for the investigation of the Poor Law in East London and Berkshire. Each appointee received detailed instructions on the information required. In all, the assistant commissioners visited 3,000 of the 15,000 parishes and townships in England and Wales. From such fieldwork came detailed reports on the workings of the Poor Law in the localities and above all in the agricultural counties of the south on which the research effort was largely concentrated. Information was also gathered by means of questionnaires administered to parish officers in town and country. Replies were received from 10 per cent of respondents, covering about 20 per cent of the population of England and Wales. Little of this material had been digested when, at the close of 1832, political pressure compelled the royal commission to release interim reports on progress and policy. Chadwick seized the initiative. While his fellow assistant commissioners produced plodding copy that was neutral and indeterminate, Chadwick proceeded to outline a comprehensive scheme of poor law reform which promised freedom from insolvency and insurrection. His report gripped the public imagination and secured his appointment as secretary to the Royal Commission.

The Poor Law Commission, though it held itself responsible for introducing 'a measure of social police' to assist the growth of a free market for labour, did not accept the Malthusian case for the total abolition of poor relief. Quite the contrary. It not only upheld the right to relief, but argued that, under certain circumstances, poor relief could be effective and efficient. In the report that followed the commissioners went on to define the principles that were appropriate to the radically reorganized system that was to become the New Poor Law [*Doc. 2*].

It was 'the mischievous ambiguity of the word *poor*' and the need to define those who came within the ambit of the Poor Law that supplied the starting-point of the report of 1834. Following the lead given by Burke and Malthus the commissioners took pains to replace the 'labouring poor' as an undifferentiated and generalizable concept by a more precise terminology in which the key distinction lay between the self-sustaining labouring classes and the recipients of relief or charity, the 'indigent' or 'pauper' classes. Poor law provision, they insisted, was reserved solely for the latter. These consisted of two categories: the impotent – i.e., the sick, the aged and widows with small children – and the able-bodied,* i.e., unemployed and underemployed men. The first remained eligible for relief in the customary manner. Not so the able-bodied for whom the terms of relief were to be redefined so as to check pauperism among those already in receipt of relief, and prevent its extension to those who had not yet become claimants. The distinction between 'poor' and 'pauper' likewise determined the conditions on which relief was offered, the famous principle of 'less eligibility' with its stipulation that the situation of the able-bodied pauper be inferior to that of the poorest independent worker. To this end, indoor relief was to be made as disagreeable as possible by vexatious regulations, want of social amenities, hard labour, poor dietaries and the imposition of strict discipline. An additional item, implied by the idea of less eligibility, was that of the 'workhouse principle'. The requirement that relief should be given to the able-bodied pauper and his family within the workhouse served to segregate the able-bodied pauper from the independent poor and underscore the differences between them. Apart from the deprivation of liberty, these included the loss of civil rights, human dignity and individual moral worth. The workhouse principle also served as a self-acting test of need. The very fact that a claimant was willing to submit to this least eligible mode of existence rendered further inquiry superfluous.

The assumption behind the redefined poor law principles was that poverty was a voluntary and therefore reversible condition. The pauper was not so much the victim as the perpetrator of his own distress. Poverty, the commissioners insisted, arose from 'fraud, indolence or improvidence'. The abolition of outdoor relief and creation of a deterrent poor law system, it was thought, would force the pauper from the workhouse to find whatever employment he could in the open market. Less eligibility in this context was also the realization of a utilitarian* ideal, being the principal means for the assimilation of the self-interest of the labourer with the common good. But, as several scholars have noted, it was based upon the abdication rather than 'the reign of fact'. In spite of the primacy accorded to rational scientific inquiry in Benthamite social theory, Chadwick had reached his conclusions in advance of the evidence. The social research undertaken by the Royal Commission on the Poor Laws was drawn upon selectively in defence of a preconceived project. Policy, in short, had become the determinant rather than the outcome of empirical inquiry [37].

This was not the only defect in Chadwick's report. The reformed Poor Law, although inclusive in its terminology, addressed rural rather than urban industrial requirements. Involuntary unemployment caused by movements in the trade cycle or labour displacement due to the mechanization of industry were not mentioned. Confident assertions on the availability of work for all who wanted it were, however, called into question by the prominence given to schemes of overseas and internal migration. Surprising, too, was the failure to abolish the settlement laws. Here tradition took precedence over consistency. In consequence, removals and the threat thereof blighted the lives of working people in town and country throughout the nineteenth century [53]. The continuing importance of locality in poor relief administration highlights the prominence of local government as an insuperable obstacle to the creation of a centrally funded national Poor Law.

Contemporary presumptions about male and female roles in the provision of relief were equally important. Policy makers like Senior and Chadwick assumed that the stable two-parent family, dependent upon the male breadwinner, was the norm. Raising the earnings of husbands and fathers was the means to maintain women and children above subsistence, and this the application of a deterrent Poor Law was sure to secure. This rather abstract view of poverty ill-accorded with industrial realities and bore little relationship to the situation of large numbers of deserted or abandoned women who struggled to sustain themselves and their dependents on starvation wages.

THE NEW POOR LAW, IMPLEMENTATION

The Poor Law Amendment Act of 1834, embodied the principal recommendations of the Royal Commission's Report and provided for the creation of a national system of poor-law administration. At the local level parishes were reorganized into poor law unions with resources sufficient to maintain a well regulated workhouse with elected boards of guardians and paid permanent officials. Each parish remained responsible for the maintenance of its own paupers and, until the 1860s, no consideration was given to the inequality of burdens as between poor and rich parishes within the same union [142]. Overseeing all was a central board of three Poor Law Commissioners, guided by Secretary Edwin Chadwick and supported by an inspectorate of assistant commissioners, which sought to impose uniformity of standards and practices through numerous regulations, orders and directives. To prevent the intrusion of party politics, the Poor Law Commission was made independent of parliament without accountability or representation.

The three-man Poor Law Commission, set up to supervise the administration of the new law, despatched a number of assistant commissioners around the country to group parishes into poor law unions, assist the formation of boards of guardians and, where appropriate, to advise on the building of new workhouses. Its authority was strictly limited. It could draw up rules and regulations and monitor their implementation, but lacked effective powers of enforcement. Its negative powers of control, though, were considerable; the central authority could veto unsuitable appointments, disallow certain kinds of building and expenditure, standardize administrative and accounting procedures, determine dietaries and even regulate the strength of workhouse porridge. Its influence was diminished partly by the absence of an accountable minister to defend the Commission against the popular criticisms that were voiced against it in parliament but also by the internal divisions for which Chadwick was in no small part responsible. Miffed at the permanent secretaryship he had received in place of the central commissioner appointment he coveted, Chadwick failed to establish effective working relationships within the new body and was rapidly frozen out of its proceedings.

The organization of the new poor law unions, though it proceeded with great rapidity, was partial in its coverage. Excluded were the parishes and unions administered under local acts or Gilbert's Act of 1782.* The Poor Law Amendment Act of 1834 included no powers to secure the dissolution or incorporation of those bodies within the reorganized national system of public relief. The exclusions were significant. Twenty-two years after the passage of the Poor Law Amendment Act, twelve of the fifty most populous parishes or unions in England and Wales still operated under local acts. The Poor Law Board whittled away their autonomy. Southampton, Bristol and Exeter were brought under central control in the 1850s; Chester and Norwich succumbed in the 1860s as, finally, did the hitherto resistant Metropolitan parishes [99].

Poor law policy after 1834 had two priorities. The first was directed at the transfer of the surplus population from the glutted countryside to the new industrial districts where labour was scarce and opportunity plentiful. The second was concerned with safeguarding the urban ratepayer from the intolerable support costs that could arise from sudden surges of rural settlers. The workhouse answered the first priority; removals under the settlement laws the second. We shall look at each in turn.

The New Poor Law thus proceeded with the brute repression of able-bodied male pauperism and reduction of rates coupled with a vigorous programme of workhouse construction [163]. The two went hand in glove as it was impossible to abolish outdoor relief unless there were workhouses to receive the able-bodied applicants who required assistance. The vast majority of the new poor law unions had erected a new workhouse before 1870. The assault on relief practices was equally vigorous. The Outdoor Labour Test Order of 1842, which made outdoor relief conditional upon the performance of task work, enabled unions whose building programmes were incomplete to uphold the spirit of the New Poor Law. In unions where workhouse accommodation was insufficient claimants would thus be required to work in the labour yards for their relief payments. The Outdoor Relief Prohibitory Order of 1844 was directed at the exclusion of unemployed, underemployed and poorly-paid able-bodied men. The General Outdoor Relief Regulation Order of 1852 extended the labour test and, for the first time, made able-bodied women subject to it [*Docs. 3* and *6*]. The effect of these measures upon local relief practices remains controversial (see Chapter 6, pp. 85–6). Their influence upon public finance is less contentious. Poor rates fell and expenditure stabilized. In the first decade of the New Poor Law, poor rates across the country fell to between £4.5 and £5 million per annum and for the next twenty years thereafter fluctuated between £5 million and £6 million.

Powers of removal under the laws of settlement were thought of as a necessary complement to the abolition of outdoor relief and pursuit of deterrence. An estimated 40,000 paupers were removed from their place of residence to their place of settlement [i.e. to the parish to which they legally belonged by birth or marriage] in England and Wales in 1840, and although numbers fell thereafter some 12,000 pauper removals took place as late as 1907. The threat of removal deterred applications for relief and was the means by which urban parishes in periods of trade depression 'sought to protect themselves against a run on their rates' [*155 p. 38*]. In theory, then, removals were the chief instrument by which an urban union could regulate the size of the dependent population and protect itself against increased poor rates. In practice, the process was cumbersome and costly and used selectively. The problem was complicated by the custom which had grown up under the Old Poor Law by which rural parishes agreed to grant outdoor relief to persons belonging to them by settlement, who were residing elsewhere. 'Non-resident' relief, as this form of assistance was known, was thought to be humane, cheaper and more convenient than the cost of repatriation. In 1846 it was estimated that 82,249 persons were in receipt of non-resident relief in England and Wales.

Progress, then, was uneven. It was slowed by inequalities in the apportionment of the costs of poor relief as between the town and the countryside and by the interests and outlook of boards of guardians whose perspective and commitments often conflicted with those of the Poor Law Commission. Guardians, moreover, were not always driven by a mindless concern for economy. They also understood the circumstances and temper of their communities much better than did the men in London. Benthamite ideas of poverty and its treatment cut no ice with local administrators who preferred to operate with conventional notions of eligibility. Unions, like Carlisle, which possessed additional resources independent of the central authority, continued to classify applicants as deserving or undeserving and administered relief according to their own understanding of the moral worth of applicants. In parts of the kingdom where problems of unemployment and able-bodied male pauperism were not pressing, the New Poor Law generated little angst. In Cumberland interest was minimal; in north Yorkshire it was considered irrelevant [70, 62]. Elsewhere communities were outraged by the act of 1834 and resisted its implementation. Opposition to the introduction of the New Poor Law, which was ineffective in the agricultural districts of southern England [71], was formidable in the industrial north. Local interests resentful of centralization and bureaucracy were joined by Tory Radicals who hated the new principles of political economy and the divorce of ethics from economics, duty from social obligation, embodied in the principles of 1834.

Mobilized against the new system, too, were the industrial workers whose precarious employment made them fearful of imprisonment and subject to the terrible discipline of the 'New Bastilles', as the workhouses became known. Anti-poor law riots in Oldham, Rochdale, Todmorden, Huddersfield and Bradford in 1837 and 1838 testified to the strength of popular feeling and fuelled the growth of Chartism [111, 154, 162]. Opposition in Wales which was almost as fierce, was driven by historic antipathies to central government and a brooding resistance among labourers which found expression in the targeting of union workhouses during the Rebecca Riots* of 1843–4 [73]. Public concern, sustained by allegations and rumours of the inhuman treatment of the inmate population, came to a head in 1845 with the revelation that starving paupers had been fed on rotting bones in the Andover workhouse. The 'Three Bashaws of Somerset House' were deemed culpable. In 1847 the autonomous Poor Law Commission was replaced by a Poor Law Board that was responsible to parliament and headed by a minister of the Crown. In 1871 the Poor Law Board was itself superseded by the newly-created Local Government Board whose president was usually a Cabinet minister. Throughout all these changes the establishment created by the Poor Law Amendment Act remained pretty much intact with a top-down management structure staffed by secretaries, legal advisers and inspectors offering direction and advice to the elected guardians of some 646 poor law unions in England and Wales.

The new boards of guardians were elected on a restricted property-based franchise and their tax powers were separated from the local authorities in order to prevent extravagance. The property qualification, which excluded women and manual workers, was abolished in 1894. But by then the pattern of local politics was well-established. Turnout at guardian elections was derisory, small-propertied interests were dominant and ratepayer pressure easily applied to hold down local expenditure. The downward squeeze on relief was limited only by the legal requirement that the poor law authorities intervene to prevent the destitute dying from starvation. Negligent authorities exposed their relieving officer to a charge of murder. For the rest, there were few incentives to exceed minimum standards of provision. Central government offered no financial support to encourage improvements and the central authority could advise but not compel guardians in respect of local management and administration [139, 150].

WOMEN AND THE POOR LAW

Time was, and not so long ago, when studies of the origins of modern social policy were framed almost exclusively in terms of class division. No longer. Women, it is now recognized, were more dependent than men upon relief under the New Poor Law. Women, too, made a signal contribution to poor law administration and poor law reform. The space available for women's participation in public life, though limited, was not insignificant [132]. Situated in voluntary action and local government, it enabled women to influence poor law administration as charity workers and (from 1894 onwards) as elected women guardians* and members of special committees and conferences [87]. Voluntary work also served as a training ground for public service. Beatrice Webb,* Helen Bosanquet,* or the equally remarkable Clara Collet,* all served their apprenticeships in social research in the private sector. Clara Collet went on to a distinguished career in the civil service while Bosanquet and Webb went on to write the Majority and Minority Reports of the Royal Commission on the Poor Laws of 1905–9 on which they served with equal distinction [145]. That they played any role at all is surprising. As we noted earlier, the New Poor Law was framed around a set of assumptions that all served to marginalize the position of women. Historians are now increasingly interested in the further exploration of the ways in which gender (i.e. the cultural construction of male and female social roles) has influenced the provision of welfare.

The Poor Law Commissioners of 1834 were preoccupied with the problem of the able-bodied unemployed male. The condition of the female population was of no concern. Women were on the whole assumed to be non-wage earning dependents. That women's earnings were critical to the family economy, or that many were heads of one-parent families, did not register. Wives, for example, had no autonomous existence but were compelled to follow their husbands into the workhouse. A destitute wife might be refused entry if her spouse declined to enter and detained if he refused to leave. The wife of a non-able-bodied pauper received the same classification whatever her physical condition and she, too, became a pauper even if he alone was the recipient of medical assistance. Women's position in respect of settlement was no less derivative. Widows or deserted wives who sought relief in a city to which they had removed for work were liable to be deported to the parish of their husband's birth as the only place that had an obligation to assist them. The gendered assumptions of the New Poor Law were highlighted by the treatment of bastardy. Unmarried mothers, it was decided, were to bear the shame of their offspring alone. No attempt would be made by the poor law authorities to sue the putative fathers for maintenance on the grounds that, to have done so, would serve 'to extend the rights of matrimony to the unqualified and undeserving'. The outcry against public support of a dual standard of sexual morality was such that the regulation had to be abandoned and remedial legislation enacted. The Poor Law Amendment Act of 1844 thus enabled the unmarried mother to sue the putative father for an affiliation order in a magistrates court and empowered the guardians to proceed against him for maintenance of the mother and child [95].

Which had the higher priority: motherhood or work? Neither the central authority nor local boards of guardians could agree on a uniform policy towards women. The former thought that relief policy should underpin the integrity of the family; the latter emphasized the rights of the child and the tolerance of the ratepayer. Local guardians and relieving officers often entertained a low opinion of mothers in distress and considered institutional care preferable to outdoor relief which, it was also thought, weakened the working-class father's sense of family commitment. Outdoor relief, when granted, had to be minimal so as not to offend ratepayer sensibilities. Confusion reigned. A mother applying for relief never knew what to expect. All of her children might be received into workhouse schools. Equally, indoor relief might be confined to one child to allow her to work and care for the rest. Wage supplements were available in some unions to permit the combination of part-time work with family maintenance. More generally, she was likely to have been the recipient of inadequate amounts of relief which enabled her to scrape by at enormous cost to her health and that of her children.

Rising costs prompted reform. The resultant shift in poor law policy in 1869–71 is the subject of the next two sections. All we need note at present is that it involved an attempt to reallocate responsibilities between the Poor Law and private benevolence so as to relieve poor law expenditure of the burden of the 'deserving poor' and facilitate the curtailment of outdoor relief. Women, who accounted for the bulk of the recipients of poor relief, became one of the principal targets in the cut-backs that followed [*Doc. 11*]. Unemployed women were for the first time required to shift for themselves as, in theory, were unemployed men. Able-bodied single women were forced to search for work and denied relief except on a labour test. Oakum picking (i.e., picking at old matted ropes used for caulking ships) rather than useful work was also preferred on the grounds that the workhouse might otherwise be perceived as insufficiently deterrent. Mothers, too, were squeezed. Outrelief was denied to those with one dependent child and children removed from those with more. Deserted wives were denied relief for the first twelve months of their desertion. For all that, the conditions which made outrelief necessary could not be dismissed no matter how many circulars and regulations bade them disappear. Whatever the pressure from Whitehall for tighter administration, guardians knew that applicants required assistance even if there were no resources for adequate relief. The screw, though, could always withstand another turn. Increasingly outdoor relief became dependent upon character and conduct and was denied to those whose habits were deemed intemperate, improvident, immoral, or insanitary [22]. These arrangements were arbitrary, unfair and inefficient. They were not the cause of poverty but they made the experience a damned sight worse.

CHARITY AND THE POOR LAW

The deterrent character of the New Poor Law was reinforced by the narrow financial base on which its activities rested. In spite of the newly-created poor law unions, the parochial basis of raising revenue from the rates remained unchanged. Rates were a charge levied compulsorily by the parish, the proceeds of which were applicable to the upkeep of the poor. They were leviable on the basis of an assessment made normally upon the occupier in respect of the net annual value of occupied property. Valuation of property for this purpose was wanting in uniformity, regularity and fairness. Industrial and commercial wealth was, in consequence, too lightly taxed or not taxed at all. In the large towns manufacturing and mercantile wealth paid an insignificant amount to the relief of the poor leaving the burden to be borne by those of modest means.

Local assessment also gave rise to enormous differences in the rate yield between parishes with large impoverished populations and those where wealth resided. In the absence of an equalizing mechanism, the rich districts escaped from contributing to the costs of the poorer districts. Failure to reform the rating system in 1834 led to considerable variation in local provision in line with the particular circumstances and differing capacities of poor law authorities. The balance between outdoor and indoor relief and the role performed by the workhouse, in consequence, owed less to any alleged personal meanness of the guardians than to the affluence or poverty of the resident population and the size of the ratepayer base. The poor rate, the largest direct tax levied upon all householders, was a regressive form of taxation the incidence of which was distributed unequally with the poorest districts bearing the heaviest burdens [69, 74]. When coinciding with a downturn in the trade cycle, high prices and wintry weather these disparities were likely as not to create a crisis in poor relief as, for example, occurred in East London in 1855, 1860–1 and in 1866–67 when the collapse of the Poor Law provoked food riots and mass refusals to pay the rates [50].

Involved here was something more than the technicalities of local finance. Contemporaries connected the maldistribution of rateable burdens with problems of class separation and the demoralization of the honest poor. The flight of the rich from the poorer districts was held to have upset the balance between charity and the Poor Law and created space for the 'clever pauper' to occupy. The scope for such activity was facilitated by the self-exclusion from the New Poor Law of eleven metropolitan parishes who preferred to administer poor relief under local acts. In the absence of a resident gentry, poor law administration had become corrupted by self-seeking officers, hard-pressed ratepayers and under-resourced authorities who were too ready to dump the cost of poor relief upon diverse charities. The indiscriminate alms-giving of these bodies, it was thought, was exploited by crafty cadgers whose subversive example threatened the self-supporting elements above them [63].

The breakdown of the poor law and the disorders that accompanied it underscored the need for rating reform. Improving measures included the streamlining of valuation procedures so as to eliminate waste and secure uniformity of assessments within and between parishes. Steps were also taken to redistribute the rate burden more fairly. These arose directly from the additional burden imposed upon urban ratepayers by the Poor Removal Act of 1846, which made widows and those who had been resident for five years wholly irremovable and in so doing transferred the cost of relief from the countryside to the towns, particularly those that were popular with rural migrants. The strains and stresses created by the resultant reallocation of costs contributed to the crisis of the metropolitan Poor Law and so to further enactments. Chief among them were the Irremovability Act of 1861 and the Union Chargeability Act of 1865. The former established the principle that rateable values rather than relief expenditure, i.e. property rather than poverty, should supply the basis of parish contributions to the common expenses of the union. The latter required a uniform rate throughout each poor law union and obliged wealthier parishes to contribute to the costs of relief in poorer parishes. London's special problems were addressed by the Metropolitan Poor Act of 1867 which provided for the creation of a Common Poor Fund (for the construction and maintenance of workhouses) to which each union was to contribute in accordance with its rateable value. By this act, too, the separate local act parishes were finally brought under the terms of the Poor Law Amendment Act of 1834 and new boards of guardians elected in the expectation that laxity would thereby be curbed. The Poor Law Board also acquired powers to nominate their own members to the London guardians in order to eliminate indiscriminate alms giving, sentimentality and inefficiency [61, 38, 48].

The confusion of charity with poor relief undermined the distinction between the deserving and undeserving poor and contributed to the relentless rise in poor law expenditure. A sharp reduction in outdoor relief was deemed essential to the restoration of the proper balance between charity and the Poor Law. The situation required a clear restatement of the principles of state and voluntary action and firm measures taken to co-ordinate the work of both sectors. By such means the demoralization encouraged by the clever pauper might be checked and the creeping assumption of a right to public relief in aid of wages halted. Such was the thinking behind the memorandum of 1869 issued by George Goschen, President of the Local Government Board [*Doc. 9*]. The new initiative looked to the Charity Organization Society as the co-ordinating agency for private charity.

The COS was founded in 1869 as the Society for Organizing Charitable Relief and Repressing Mendicity. It sought to prevent duplication, waste and inefficiency in the distribution of charitable resources, to formulate and apply scientific methods of social casework and to counsel, advise and reform the recipients of charity so that they might resume their place among the self-reliant classes. The powers of the Poor Law Board to nominate COS supporters as guardians, it was anticipated, would help to maintain approved standards of poor law administration and secure the necessary collaboration between public and private agencies. Personal investigation of individual applicants was expected to separate the genuine cases of destitution from the get-on element. The former were deemed suitable for poor law assistance. The latter, it was hoped, might be prevailed upon to foresake mendicancy for labour thereby enabling the demoralized poor to regain an appetite for thrift and self-help. Close casework also offered a chance to restore the deference and submission which, it was believed, came from benign contact between rich and poor.

The COS and its members have been likened to a new urban squirearchy. Drawn from the elite of the professional classes – clergy, lawyers, doctors, civil servants and the armed forces – their view of charity as a science requiring specialized knowledge and expertize reflected their social origins. Upon their education and vocational training rested their claims to leadership and deference [63]. In the assertion of these claims they were extraordinarily successful. Historians now think that the COS was a bit of a fraud. Its claims to primacy in the co-ordination of charitable effort were bogus. It had neither the cash nor the personnel to sustain its relief strategies let alone hold its own in partnership with the Poor Law [127]. Still, it is difficult to deny that COS members did punch well above their weight. The poor may have abused them as victims rather than clients, but not the governing classes who readily promoted them to official inquiries and other positions of influence [133].

The leading lights of the COS, Octavia Hill (1838–1912), Charles Bosanquet, Edward Denison (1840–1870) and their indefatigable secretary C.S. Loch (1849–1923), all believed that the moral improvement of the masses, the basis of all future progress, could only be achieved by the rigorous enforcement of the principles of 1834. The COS proved to be the staunchest of allies in the crusade against outdoor relief that was triggered by the Goschen memorandum. The crusade, directed by the Local Government Board, was well received by ratepayers and boards of guardians. The restriction of outdoor relief, it was hoped, would reduce expenditure and relieve the rates [*Doc. 10*]. But to succeed, the campaign required capital expenditure to provide workhouses at an acceptable standard. The shift to local taxation based upon rateable values rather than expenditure on poor relief and the increase in rateable values during the 1860s favoured such a move. The enlarged tax base created by the legislation of 1861–66 (see above p. 21) gave the wealthier parishes, who were now compelled to make substantial contributions to relief costs, a greater interest in economy. The increase in effective rateable values made possible the improvement in workhouse facilities that was necessary to prevent the build-up of resistance to the curbing of out-relief [48, 69, 74].

As a cost-cutting exercise that campaign was a considerable success. Relief rolls were slashed. The number on outdoor relief fell steadily from 39.1 outdoor paupers per thousand of the population in 1871 to 10.5 per thousand in 1914. Between 1871 and 1876 alone 276,000 paupers, one in three of all those on outrelief, were removed from the rolls. In the attempt to reduce expenditure, extra staff were hired to ferret out imagined scroungers on the rates. Women, who accounted for the bulk of the recipients of outdoor relief, were particularly vulnerable. Previously, able-bodied widows with dependent children had been exempted from the prohibitions on outdoor relief. After 1871 they fell victim to the renewed economy drive. Pauper women were placed under close surveillance and neighbourhoods monitored to see whether single women on relief were also receiving support from the men with whom they cohabited. Mothers on outrelief were pressed to surrender their children to the workhouse and seek employment; single women were offered a labour test – cleaning the workhouse – in return for outdoor assistance. Numbers fell dramatically. Women on outrelief dropped from 166,407 in 1871 to 53,371 in 1891 [95]. The hardship and suffering concealed in these bald figures is difficult to imagine.The absorptive capacities of the labour market were illusory and charitable resources insufficient. The strict outdoor relief policy of the 1870s began to slacken in face of the severe unemployment of the 1880s. Its achievements were difficult to identify. Reductions in the overall cost of outrelief were overshadowed by the sporadic rises that accompanied the peak years of recession – 1879–80, 1886–7, 1895–6 and 1905–6 – and so contributed little to the peace of mind of the propertied classes. The possibility of a return to the practices of the unreformed Poor Law was also kept alive by the opposition of boards of guardians in which a powerful labour presence had been established. The example of West Ham and Poplar, where the influence of labour was pronounced, in particular, served to encourage certain urban boards to make more generous provision, indoor and outdoor, than the central authority intended. Most disturbing was the fact that, while the cost of outdoor relief had been falling, total poor law expenditure had been rising, and rising sharply. The cost of buildings and improvement in standards accounted for the increase.

CLASSIFICATION AND TREATMENT, 1870–1914

The repression of pauperism was the dominant but not the sole priority of social policy. From the outset Chadwick had understood that deterrence was not a sufficient basis for social assistance. His poor law project recognized non-economic sources of pauperism arising from sickness, accident, age, housing stress and intemperance. He thus included provision for a range of 'collateral aids' to accompany the less eligibility principle. The rigours of the 1834 system, directed at able-bodied, unemployed men, were not intended for the helpless poor whose special needs were readily identifiable through classification. The Royal Commission of 1834 envisaged the separation of different categories of paupers within the workhouse: the impotent (aged and infirm), children, lunatics, able-bodied men and able-bodied women. Chadwick, who advocated the construction of separate buildings for each group, was never reconciled to the indiscriminate lumping of paupers in a 'general mixed workhouse'. His thinking, neglected in the early years of the New Poor Law, was taken up after 1870 to supply the basis of a dual strategy in which institutional assistance was combined with curative and deterrent principles. Guardians were thus advised to arrange the inmate population by cause of poverty and 'character' and to create a graduated scale of comforts for each separate class, the most deserving being the best rewarded. The absence of financial assistance from central government, however, created considerable variation in the volume, design and construction of poor law buildings.

Workhouse hospitals, built in the larger urban unions, were set apart from the principal workhouse building, and often became the prime source of free medical assistance for the working population of those areas. Improved standards of health care, the fruits of medical science and more professional nursing, extended from the voluntary hospitals to the new poor law infirmaries, albeit somewhat patchily. The employment of workhouse inmates as nurses or the confusion of maternity wards with brothels were by no means exceptional even at the close of our period. However, there was more to the poor law medical service than the acquisition of resources. The implications of medical improvement, in respect of poor law reform, were just as important; for nothing proved more subversive of the principles of 1834 than illness and infirmity. The poor law medical service developed in response to special needs rather than ideological requirements. The outlines of a non-pauperizing health service were visible even before the passage of the Second Reform Act. In that time outdoor medical relief was made generally available and treatment for accidents and maternity granted without recourse to the workhouse. In 1841 Parliament had decreed that the smallpox vaccination, though administered by poor law medical officers, did not pauperize the recipient. A further breach with poor law principles came in 1852 with the recognition that inability to pay medical fees or pharmaceutical charges, whether employed or jobless, created an entitlement to outdoor treatment by the poor-law medical officer. The movement away from a pauper medical service was also hastened by the public dispensaries, that were established by the poor law unions from the 1850s onwards, and by the growing scale and professionalism of the workhouse hospitals. The connection between sickness and less eligibility was severed with the passage of the Metropolitan Poor Act of 1867 which also provided for the further separation of medical aid and pauperism. Henceforth London was organized into 'asylum districts' under the Metropolitan Asylums Board which assumed responsibility for the provision of general, specialist, isolation and mental hospitals. Finally, the granting of assistance without disfranchisement under the terms of the Medical Relief (Disqualifications Removal) Act of 1885 eliminated the stigma of the Poor Law from medical treatment and made a significant contribution to the idea of the social service state [86, 89, 93].

Institutional provision for children was no less innovative. The ambiguous status of pauper education, though resolved in defiance of the less eligibility principle – on the grounds that children were innocent and education would assist their ascent into self-maintenance – was at first limited by want of resources. Legislation of 1844, which enabled poor law unions to combine to establish District Schools, offered partial relief. New approved schools removed children from the unwholesome influence of the general mixed workhouse to distant, and not always sanitary, buildings in which control and regulation took precedence over self-development and the values of a liberal education. The building of these 'barrack schools' was halted in 1896. By that time improvement was well under way and the need for a less penal regime increasingly recognized. 'Detached' (i.e., onsite but separate) schools had been introduced and standards of teaching raised. Mind-numbing task-work, too, gave place to useful industrial training. Boys were taught a trade; girls received instruction in domestic economy. The passage of the Education Act of 1870 was the decisive influence upon poor law guardians. Henceforth, pauper children could attend the new board schools and ratepayers were relieved of a costly and inferior form of provision.

In the generation before the First World War pauper education was transformed. The vast barrack schools in which workhouse children were taught to be submissive and useful, were abandoned and the inmates transferred to the smaller units pioneered by benevolent reformers like Samuel and Henrietta Barnett* and progressive bodies like Barnardo. 'Cottage homes', with accommodation for between twelve and twenty children and their attendants, provided a more intimate and supportive setting for learning and living. Children, previously withdrawn from normal social intercourse, were encouraged to participate in the compulsory free educational system and attend ordinary schools like ordinary children. Apart from questions of cost, the shift reflected the influence of new theories of personality and the formative role of the environment in child development allied to a growing awareness of the retardative effects of barrack school provision. Graduates of these institutions, it was noted, were often wanting in self-confidence and initiative and deficient in social skills [87a]. The fostering of pauper children in working-class families, cheaper and in many respects a more suitable mode of provision, remained underdeveloped because the central authority had too few resources to supervize placements and feared that cost-conscious guardians were inclined to unload its responsibilities on to unsuitable homes [88, 94].

The special needs of the elderly also began to receive recognition. In the latter years of the queen's reign the aged poor were reclassified to become the most privileged element within the inmate population and the most deserving among the recipients of outdoor relief. Special wards were created within the main workhouse and the disciplinary regime relaxed. Apart from the discarding of the pauper's uniform, the elderly were allowed to share a room with their spouses and receive visitors. Husbands could smoke. Wives were permitted extra tea and supplementary comestibles. Those who were not in need of institutional care also became eligible for more generous assistance. Circulars issued by the Local Government Board in 1895 and 1899 advised guardians that outdoor relief should be more readily granted to the aged and deserving poor [96].

UNEMPLOYMENT AND THE POOR LAW

Nowhere was the conflict between specialization and deterrence more significant than in respect of the treatment of unemployment. The terms 'unemployed' and 'unemployment' which entered common usage during the 1880s, signalled a change in understanding of the social problem. The revision in outlook was, in part, prompted by the unexpected rise in working-class living standards in the previous fifty years or so, assisted by the downturn in prices which began in 1873 and continued unabated almost until the close of the nineteenth century. Political economy's obsession with the limits of economic growth – its fears of overpopulation and anxieties respecting the creation of a wage fund* sufficient to satisfy the needs of an expanding labour force – gave way to a more hopeful view of the possibilities of working-class advance. The working class, it was noted, was not a monolith. Indeed, contemporaries more often than not spoke of the working classes. The respectable stratum, mainly relatively well-paid craftsmen in regular employment, was increasingly welcomed as a middle class in waiting. These people were more and more recognized as rational capable beings who, through the conduct of their co-ops, mechanics institutes, friendly societies and trade unions, had shown themselves fit for further participation in public life. The extension of the franchise in 1867, while satisfying their claims to citizenship, left a 'residuum' of helpless poverty and dependence which resisted the march of progress. This was the social problem [120]. Between the respectable rate-paying householder and the paupers, casual workers and semi-criminal elements who made up the residuum there existed an unbridgeable gulf. Upon this distinction rested middle-class fears for order and social stability. Should the respectable artisan ever be reduced to the condition of the residuum, who knew what mischief might occur? It was this spectre which was raised by the deepening economic depression of the 1880s. Mass unemployment, particularly severe in London, affected workers who were anything but the stereotypical poor of contemporary social commentary. The possibility of the respectable unemployed craftsman throwing in his lot with the casual poor under the leadership of revolutionary socialism gained considerable credence after the disturbances of 1886 and 1887 when police and troops were mustered to safeguard the West End against marauding unemployed rioters [63]. It was becoming difficult to sustain the belief that unemployment was a voluntary condition and dangerous to do so.

The need for a new departure found expression in the circular issued by Joseph Chamberlain, President of the Local Government Board, on 15 March 1886. In it the leader of Liberal radicalism recommended conjoint action by the poor law guardians and local authorities to provide non-pauperizing emergency work schemes for 'steady and respectable' workers who were temporarily unemployed [*Doc. 13*]. The circular, which supplied the basis of unemployment policy for the next twenty years, prompted numerous experiments with work-creation projects – limewashing, levelling, street sweeping, roadmaking, etc. – which, while they did little for the jobless workers at whom they were directed, served to highlight the even more intractable problems arising from casual labour. Solutions included the creation of 'farm colonies', which would provide agricultural training for land settlement at home or in the Empire, and quasi-penal 'labour colonies' for the incorrigible elements who declined to participate in reclamatory schemes or were deemed incapable of benefiting from them [1, PRO/MH12/7950].

It was the need for order arising from the proliferation of work creation schemes within and outwith the Poor Law which led to the passage of the Unemployed Workmen's Act of 1905. It was prompted by the recurrence of severe unemployment in the aftermath of the Boer War and by fears of disorderly demonstrations organized by the labour movement. The Balfour administration, seeking to avoid the assumption of state responsibility for the unemployed, moved instead to improve the co-ordination of public and voluntary sectors in the metropolitan districts. Distress committees on which local authorities, poor law guardians and local charities were represented were formed in each of the London boroughs to determine the division of labour between the Poor Law and other bodies in respect of the treatment of the unemployed. A strategic and supervisory perspective was provided by a Central Unemployed Body for the whole of London which was made up of delegates elected by the various distress committees. This scheme was extended to the urban districts of England and Wales and made compulsory under the Unemployed Workmen's Act of 1905. In spite of denials that the measure amounted to a recognition of state responsibility to those without work, it was clear both to the government and its critics that boundaries had become blurred and the relationship between the Poor Law and the unemployed uncertain [119]. This is simply another way of saying that the scope and purpose of the Poor Law itself had become problematical. Were the principles of 1834 still relevant? Did they address the needs of an urban industrial society? Could deterrence remain the basis of a modern social service state? The government had no answers. A royal commission was appointed in the hope that it might produce some. It reported in 1909. But by then social policy had entered a new phase.

CONCLUSION

The theoretical basis of poor law administration, as developed in the report of 1834, was never realized in practice. Outdoor relief resisted total abolition. Part of the difficulty was economic. Workhouses with specialized provision for different categories of paupers – the young, the old, the sick and the infirm as envisaged by Senior and his colleagues – were expensive to build without financial support from central government. Guardians, responsive to local opinion, also showed no inclination to implement the principles of 1834 in industrial centres where outdoor relief was the only way of seeing unemployed workers through slack seasons or through a severe downturn in the trade cycle. Even in rural areas, the shadow cast by Speenhamland was never so large as to deter farmer guardians from seeking to sustain a reserve labour force from the proceeds of the parish chest [43]. Welsh resistance to the workhouse principle was such that the abolition of outdoor relief was too provocative to contemplate. The dilution of poor law principles had in fact begun quite early. The Outdoor Labour Test Order of 1842 which exchanged outdoor relief for hard labour – stone-breaking in specially created labour yards and oakum picking – disclosed the gap between the free market assumptions of poor law theory and industrial realities and was a tacit admission that the Poor Law could not cope with large-scale unemployment. The erroneous assumption that work would always be available to those who were willing to go out and seek it was not, however, abandoned.

The discrepancy between image and reality was in large part concealed by the contribution of philanthropy and charity to the maintenance of the poor. In London alone the income raised by charities easily exceeded the expenditure of the metropolitan poor law unions [138]. Concerns about the indiscriminate distribution of this largesse and the adverse social consequences thereof found expression in the formation of the COS and its attempts to co-ordinate the giving of alms as a supplement to the Poor Law. Recent scholarship has shown that the COS, in its everyday operations, was far less important than its supporters liked to suggest. Its resources were pitiful, its procedures cumbersome, its scales of relief inferior to those available under the Poor Law and its claims to national status illusory [127]. 'Cringe or Starve', the popular rendition of the acronym

'COS', readily expressed the gap between its caring statements and the realities of its charitable practice. It also suggested the need to recast relations between the statutory and voluntary sectors to accommodate the increased demand for social protection. The state itself was, indeed, the prime mover in this direction.

The poor law was the dominant but not the sole provider of social services. Increasingly it faced competition from central and local government. Urban municipalities, following the introduction of elected councils in 1833, proceeded by special Acts of parliament to initiate significant programmes of urban improvement and social betterment. The London County Council, formed in 1888, was equally active; central government no less so. In the workplace, in the home, in the schools its presence was becoming more pronounced. As noted earlier, the Poor Law was not uninfluenced by the growth of social intervention. In the spheres of education, for example, the national system that was created in 1870 served, albeit unwittingly, to promote the education of pauper children within the community. The treatment of the sick pointed in the same direction. In vain did the authorities try to apply the principle of less eligibility to medical treatment. It was just not feasible to reduce the level of pauper medical provision below that of the independent labourer or to force all applicants for medical relief into a workhouse. The attempt to combine deterrence and curative treatment under the auspices of a single agency failed. Specialization and deterrence were irreconcilable. There could be no movement from a framework of repression to a framework of prevention. Specialized services were hopelessly compromised by their association with the Poor Law. In the years before the First World War opinion in favour of a fresh start was making headway. The principle of public works, as endorsed by the Chamberlain Circular, was thus seized upon as implying a duty to provide work outside the Poor Law in respect of involuntary unemployment. The need for a more comprehensive social services, that was free from the taint of pauperism and better adjusted to democratic requirements had, in fact, been recognized even before the guns began to roar.

3 INSIDE THE WORKHOUSE

PAUPER PALACES

The deterrent and disciplinary functions of the New Poor Law were embodied in the design and structure of the large new workhouses that guardians were encouraged to build. The spectacle of large efficient prison-like establishments, it was thought, would create confidence among poor law personnel and strike terror among the able-bodied population. In short, the architecture of the workhouse was meant to represent the new approach to relief provision. Model plans, drawn up by Sampson Kempthorne,* were issued by the central authority for the guidance of boards of guardians. Kempthorne presented alternate designs for a two- or three-storey general mixed workhouse. The first, based upon a modified Panopticon* principle, included a Y shaped radial structure enclosed within a hexagonal boundary wall. Paupers were housed in two- or three-storey wings with day rooms on the ground floor and dormitories above. Kitchen, dining hall and chapel were accommodated in a third wing; work rooms were placed around the perimeter wall. The master's apartments, located at the centre, provided, if not for the inspection of the whole establishment, then for a view of the exercise yards that separated each of the wings. Most preferred among poor law authorities in England and Wales was Kempthorne's cruciform design. Here the walls around the workhouse assumed the shape of a square, divided up by two-storey blocks of buildings forming a plus sign; an additional wing at the front included the waiting hall, the board room and the porter's lodge. The cruciform structure, which had accommodation for between two and five hundred inmates, was readily adaptable and considerably cheaper than alternative designs. All plans for the workhouse system, however, possessed a prison-like severity; all provided for the isolation of paupers behind high walls, all had gates, locks and clocks and all expressed a new form of bureaucratic management and order [108, 134].

The division of space within the workhouse provided for the requirements of a uniform disciplinary regime. Kempthorne's designs made careful provision for the differentiation of pauper classes: dormitories and dayrooms were allocated to each sex, there were separate arrangements for children and special facilities for the sick. Not all workhouses were newly-built. The vast construction programme that took place between 1834 and 1870 included provision for the alteration and extension of existing buildings so that they, too, could apply the new principles of classification to the regulation of the inmates. Classification had three functions: the provision of treatment according to the needs of each class; deterrence and discipline; and the prevention of 'moral' contagion arising from the mixing of men with women, adults with children, sane with insane and sick with healthy. For these purposes the inmate population was arranged into seven distinct categories: men infirm through age or any other cause; able-bodied males over fifteen; boys between seven and fifteen; women infirm through age or any other cause; able-bodied females over fifteen; girls between seven and fifteen; and children under seven. The Workhouse Rules Order of 1842, which defined the foregoing, also provided for the spatial segregation of each category of pauper and prevention of communication between them.

The workhouse environment and the discipline enforced did little to stimulate the imagination. Paupers found nought for their comfort. Guardians, advised by the central authority, created a setting that was positively repellent. Furniture was minimal and furnishings coarse; walls were bare and amenities non-existent. Adults had nothing to read and children nothing to play with. And the day was long. Summoned by bells, the pauper rose at 5 a.m. in summer and at 7 o'clock in winter. Prayers preceded breakfast and work began at 7 a.m. in summer and 8 a.m. in winter. There was an hour's break at midday after which work resumed until 6 p.m. Supper was followed by evening prayers and at 8 p.m. the pauper went to bed. No labour, apart from household work and cooking, was performed on Sunday, Christmas Day and Good Friday. Recreation was minimal. Cards and games of chance were proscribed and smoking forbidden. Inmates were ordinarily confined within the workhouse walls.

For one class of inmates, however, the regime was even more repressive. Vagrants, considered less deserving than the settled poor, were separated from the generality of paupers to pass the night in the casual ward. Their diet was inferior to that of the regular inmates while the work required of them was just as severe. They arrived late in the afternoon and milled around the workhouse gates waiting for admission – 4 p.m. in winter and 6 p.m. in summer. In due course, they were joined by the 'tramp major', usually a trusted inmate or ex-tramp, who searched them and removed their personal belongings. Inside they encountered seasonal workers who lodged overnight to save money and those of no fixed abode who roamed around town and came to the casual ward to avoid imprisonment under the Vagrancy Act of 1824.* In better regulated wards casuals were stripped, bathed and their clothes disinfected. A bread and water supper was then served. Accommodation was sparse and insanitary conditions by no means uncommon. Often they lay on straw and floor in some shed or outhouse and were sent on their way the following morning without breakfast. Getting shot of them was, for the workhouse authorities, the principal consideration. In the eyes of the respectable classes the homeless and workless who congregated in the casual wards occupied a borderland between indigence and criminality. These, the lowest of the low, were thought of as turbulent disease-ridden desperadoes who were beyond reform and redemption. Recruits to the 'dangerous classes', they constituted a hard core of dissolute parasites who ought to be transported or incarcerated within remote labour colonies and segregated from society proper. Victorian attitudes to the vagrants and the casual poor* – and the two were easily elided in contemporary thinking – were more than an expression of a new-fangled bourgeois deterrence. They were also a restatement of a coercive tradition of poor relief that had its origins in the Tudor legislation of the sixteenth century.

The authorities, reluctant to consider the possibility of a close connection between unemployment and vagrancy or to admit that vagrancy and pauperism were not unrelated, concentrated their efforts upon repression. London led the way. The Houseless Poor Act of 1864 provided for a network of improved casual wards, centrally funded, into which the homeless poor were to be driven by police action. Powers of detention were introduced in 1871 and extended in 1882. Labour was made compulsory and tasks suitably deterrent. Casuals who refused to work became liable to imprisonment. The effect of all this seems minimal. The departmental committee which examined the problem in 1904 concluded that vagrants were in general a bunch of good-for-nothing layabouts who would not exist but for indiscriminate charity and that the best solution was to transfer them from the Poor Law to police control. Neither reformation nor rehabilitation was required of the vagrant; getting him off the parish and onto the road was enough [161].

THE INMATE POPULATION

What kinds of people entered the workhouse? Apart from their destitution, what is known of their age, civil condition and previous occupation? How long did they stay and how many times were they readmitted? The available evidence, baldly summarized, shows an inmate population made up of transient and semi-permanent elements. The former constituted a shifting body of young people for whom the workhouse was a temporary solution to a local emergency or personal crisis. Turnover in this sector was very high and multiple admissions not uncommon. Such people moved in and out of the workhouse during the course of the year in line with the seasonality of production. Although through-put was sometimes inflated by exceptional distress caused by epidemics, severe winters or the disruption of a local industry, the general pattern was for the workhouse to fill up in winter when work was scarce and empty in summer when jobs were plentiful [17].

Parliamentary returns for 1861 and 1871 indicate that about a fifth of inmates had lived in the workhouse for upwards of five years. Most long-term residents were admitted because they were old and infirm or young and dependent. The workhouse provided a home for the aged, the decrepit and the geriatric and a hospital for those who were temporarily or chronically sick. These, the non-able-bodied, accounted for up to one-half of all paupers during the nineteenth century. Extended care within the workhouse also arose from disability and mental illness. The proportion of pauper lunatics rose dramatically in the second half of the nineteenth century. In 1842 one in one hundred paupers was classed as insane but by 1910 the proportion had risen to one in every eight paupers [163].

Elderly men were particularly prominent among the inmate population. Old women, being less helpless than old men, were more likely to remain with their families. So long as they could perform household duties and take care of children, they were an asset unlike old men who, as a result of the sexual division of labour, were generally less useful around the house. Fathers as disciplinarians may also have been less loved than mothers and more readily placed in an institution once they had become a burden to their families. Children, who made up between a quarter and a two-fifths of all paupers throughout the period of our study, were also a core component of the long stay population. Their circumstances varied. Most were orphaned or abandoned, many were sick and infirm and large numbers were the illegitimate offspring of other inmates. These were likely to pass their childhood and youth in the workhouse unlike the children of able-bodied paupers who came and went with the seasons [87a].

The refusal of outdoor relief to unsupported women made them a significant element of the inmate population. Among them were deserted wives, widows with children and out of work servants. Included, too, were large numbers of 'fallen women', unmarried mothers, prostitutes and those who for one reason and another had lost their character and place in society. The reclamation of these moral outcasts provided the spur to an enormous amount of philanthropic activity. The chosen few might, in consequence, secure a place as a domestic in a decent home. The less fortunate remained subject to a discriminatory regime in which they were allocated the routine drudgery roles performed by able-bodied female inmates but with additional deprivations as punishment for their transgressions [95].

The workhouse, then, was always something more than a test of destitution for the able-bodied. It was also the continuing home for a large number of helpless persons in a common regimen and under one management. The incompatibility of its mutiple roles – general hospital, almshouse, foundling house, maternity home, schoolhouse, lunatic asylum, blind home, deaf and dumb asylum, home for mental defectives – made for tense and stressful relations between inmates and staff alike.

WORKHOUSE STAFF

Each workhouse was a world unto itself. Enclosed within high walls and secluded from the community, it was administered by a staff of salaried officers. Apart from the master and matron, the minimal workhouse establishment included a chaplain, medical officer, schoolteacher, nurse and porter. In the larger urban unions the master might also be assisted by a clerk or assistant master to keep the account books. Some lived in; others were non-resident. Non-resident officers included the workhouse chaplain, schoolteacher and porter.

The principal officer, the master, acted as general manager; matron was responsible for the female paupers and supervised the domestic work of the house. Master and matron, who were invariably married and without dependent children, had their own apartment and were often attended by pauper servants in defiance of the central authority. The couple, who came without formal training, were overworked, underpaid and unsupervised by the guardians by whom they were appointed. Masters were responsible for the discipline and economy of the institution and were formidable figures. Whether cruel or kind, they enjoyed enormous power over workhouse staff and inmates. Masters could deny entry to anyone who came without warning, including the guardians themselves. Staff could not leave the house without the master's permission. Inmates could please themselves, but whether workhouse life was tolerable or tyrannical depended upon the ways in which masters chose to exercise their authority. The master's task was primarily to enforce industry, order, punctuality, and cleanliness and also to keep detailed accounts of workhouse stores and property. His responsibilities towards the inmates did not extend much beyond the reading of prayers and supervision of grace before meals [24].

Workhouse welfare duties were parcelled out among medical officers and schoolteachers. The spiritual welfare of the inmates was the responsibility of the workhouse chaplain, a part-time position, usually undertaken by a curate keen to supplement his stipend. The chaplain was expected to officiate at a Sunday service, catechize the children once a month, comfort the sick and minister to the dying. Socially he was a cut above the workhouse medical officer. The 'parish doctor', who combined workhouse service with private practice, was generally regarded as no better than a struggling tradesman. Hired on a short-term contract, he had to supply all drugs and medical appliances from his own salary. He was subservient to the guardians and often under the thumb of economically-minded masters who frequently ignored or countermanded his recommendations on patient care. The workhouse medical officer also differed from his compeers in that his professional duties were closely allied with the maintenance of workhouse discipline. Classification not only established the state of health of individual paupers, but also determined their work, diet and fitness to receive punishment. Although some doctors found such duties disagreeable, the majority appear to have shared the prevalent moral assumptions on the nature of pauperism. Its taint, however, was not confined to the patient. The lowly status of the workhouse medical officer was reinforced by the range of his cases and limited resources at his disposal. Apart from routine sickness, he received the chronic, venereal and infectious cases that the voluntary hospitals declined to treat. Denied the prestige associated with teaching and research, underfunded and short on drugs and equipment, workhouse medicine remained bottom of the professional hierarchy, a residual service rather than an embryonic national health service [17].

Until the 1860s conditions in workhouse infirmaries were scandalous. Improvement followed the public outcry brought about by the revelations of the *Lancet* and the campaign joined by Dickens, Mill and members of the medical profession. Apart from the equalization of the rate burden, the Metropolitan Poor Act of 1867 provided for the transfer of lunatic, fever and smallpox cases from workhouse infirmaries to separate institutions managed by the newly constituted Metropolitan Asylums Board. Improved facilities, however, were not accompanied by a corresponding improvement in standards of health care. The poor law medical service remained a Cinderella service staffed by second-rate doctors and untrained nurses. Poor law infirmaries could not compete with the voluntary hospitals in recruiting trained nurses, who were few in number and repelled by the inferior pay and inadequate living quarters of the workhouse. The sick poor in consequence relied upon the ministrations of pauper nurses who received extra rations and sometimes alcohol for their services. Nurses, paid or unpaid, were supervised by matron and treated like servants rather than health care professionals. More often than not they were mere drudges, on call day and night, eating and sleeping in the same ward as their patients, without capability, confidence or commitment [89, 90].

The parish teacher, like the parish doctor, was a lowly sort, who was overworked and underpaid, and confused by the conflict arising from the pursuit of a non-deterrent vocation within a less eligible environment. Poor law teachers were a sorry lot who were kept firmly under the master's control. They were expected not only to perform as teachers but also to act as nursemaids and assume responsibility for the cleanliness and appearance of their charges. Poorly qualified, they were depressed by their isolation and lack of holidays and dejected by their ill-use as general attendants [17]. Still, their situation was marginally better than that of the porter who occupied the lowest position among workhouse officers. His task was to man the workhouse gate, prevent unauthorized entry except of applicants for relief and to search for prohibited items such as tobacco and intoxicating drink. Porters, like schoolmasters and schoolmistresses were generally expected to be single and devote their waking hours to the institution. They came to constitute a fraught community living together but remaining alone, sharing little except the exercise of power over a captive audience just as the master exercised power over them. Truly, they made the institution as they were made by it.

WORKHOUSE DISCIPLINE

Becoming an inmate was a carefully regulated process that was designed to diminish individuality and impress upon entrants the power and authority of the workhouse staff. 'The environment thus created', wrote Sidney and Beatrice Webb,* 'starved both the will and the intelligence, and forced the pauper into a condition of blank-mindedness. By this means it was intended that no destitute person still capable of exerting or of enjoying himself, with the merest shred of mental faculty or mental desire, would consent to remain in the workhouse a day longer than he could help' [24 *p. 82*]. The master had to admit all persons who presented the proper order, at whatever hour of the day or night. Whether drunk or sober the applicant could not be denied. The pauper, following a summary appearance before the board of guardians, was admitted with his family into the receiving or probationary ward to await medical examination and classification. The family was separated, husbands from wives, children from parents. Separation was a fundamental feature of the disciplinary regime. It was based on the assumption that the pauper had relinquished responsibility for the maintenance of his family and should therefore be parted from them. The aged and infirm were not in theory exempted on the basis that the expectation of public relief would serve as a disincentive to the formation of provident and industrious habits early in life. Children were taken from their mothers at the age of seven and sent to distant pauper schools. Control over appearance, too, was removed. Paupers, once bathed and disinfected, were compelled to wear the distinctive uniform of the workhouse to broadcast their status and advertize their shame. Razors were prohibited. Men shaved once a week. Staff looked on while inmates took their weekly bath. Newcomers were packed into a dormitory with others of the same class. There was no space for small possessions, lockers, comforts – anything, in fact, which provided scope for individual identity and personal expression. At bedtime clothes were strewn across the bed or stuffed under it [134].

Inmates, if classed as able-bodied, were set to work. Cost-conscious guardians, ever keen to please the ratepayers, promptly set women and children on general household service in laundries, kitchens, sick wards and infirmaries. The purpose of pauper production, however, centred on rehabilitation and restoration of independence rather than the maximizing of profit. It followed that the rewards of such industry should not exceed the cost of maintenance otherwise it would weaken the will to compete in the labour market. The problem was to find work that was suitable and economical to perform. Failing to do so, the guardians fell back on forms of labour that were punishing and without pride, dignity or any other satisfaction. Inmates were engaged on useless tasks which placed the pauper on a par with the convict and contributed to the degradation of each. Women made sacks or shredded their hands picking at oakum while elderly men bent their backs in the labour yards. Some chopped wood for a non-existent retail market while others broke stone to create rubble for use in the making and repair of roads. The least fortunate trudged round and round turning a corn-grinding capstan to produce inferior flour for workhouse bread. Work thus became a source of deterrence rather than self-respect. Its civilizing qualities were debased and its possibilities as a form of self-expression diminished [24, 25].

Diet, too, served to discipline and deter. Local dietaries were vetted by the central authority to prevent extravagance and safeguard nutritional standards. Of equal concern was the striking of a balance between the requirements of less eligibility and pauper starvation. Guardians, though popularly suspected of erring on the side of the latter, looked to a fixed and unvarying diet that sustained life but gave no pleasure, to a diet that was deficient in taste rather than in quantity. Imaginations were not overtaxed by the preparation of menus. Guardians might choose from one of the six model diets recommended by the Poor Law Board. These were graded by the age and sex of inmates. Women received less bread and meat than men. The able-bodied received the plainest fare. The monotony in all cases was striking. Diet No. 3, for example, provided for a seven-day cycle in which the able-bodied male generally breakfasted on gruel* and bread, lunched on cheese and bread and supped on cheese and bread. Soup and bread was served once, and once a week dinner consisted of meat and potatoes and of bacon and potatoes. Water was the only drink permitted; tea, along with butter and sugar, was a privilege available to the elderly; beer was proscribed. Children over the age of nine were classed as women for catering purposes; smaller children received smaller portions of the adult menu at dinner time with milk substituting for gruel at breakfast and cheese at supper. The poor law inspectorate was ever alert to deviant extras, like fresh vegetables, or even salt, and keen to remove them in the interests of a repressive uniformity. Regimented feeding arrangements served a similar purpose. From 1835 to 1842 meals were taken in silence and although the rule was relaxed thereafter, meal times remained an exercise in deterrence. Lined up and marched to the hall, inmates were sometimes compelled to wait their turn while each portion was weighed so that, by the time they were seated at table, hot food had turned cold. It was not the only way in which food was spoilt. Supplies were often adulterated, cooking indifferent and cutlery an optional extra [17, 134].

Deterrent principles did not in theory apply to pauper children. Children, though not held responsible for their indigence, could not be allowed a situation superior to that of the independent labourer without tempting the latter to offload his children onto the parish. Children, it was agreed, should receive education, as its denial deprived them of the possibility of ever taking their place as self-supporting members of the community. The form of provision, however, should not be prejudicial to the good order and discipline of the workhouse. The solution was found in treating the child as though he were an adult, ignoring the fact that, unlike them, he could not leave the house at will, and would be forcibly returned if he tried to do so. The results were disastrous for the personal development of the child who rapidly became institutionalized and unable to cope with the unwalled world beyond the workhouse. The discipline enforced in the schoolroom was not such as to make them want to try. The liberal use of corporal punishments, the confinement of alleged wrongdoers to a darkened room during the night together with comparable forms of abuse, were calculated to produce docility rather than the mental and moral improvement that were the stated aims of the central authority. Masters, too, often placed considerations of economy and utility above all others. The priority which they assigned to industrial training often meant that children were withdrawn from the classroom and put on light work around the workhouse or apprenticed at the age of nine to any workman who was prepared to take them [91]. The wider concept of education held by the Poor Law Commission found expression in the district schools which reduced the moral 'contagion' of the workhouse in general and the adverse influence of the master in particular. Here, too, discipline was less arbitrary and the staff trained. The more hopeful trend, however, began with the transfer of children from workhouse schools to local elementary schools, a process set in motion by the passage of the Education Act of 1870 [87a].

INMATES AND INDISCIPLINE

Images of the poor are often contradictory. Victorian viewpoints were varied. Paupers were frequently represented as deviant, depressed marginal sorts who were helpless, hopeless and harmless. These were people who had had the stuffing knocked out of them and lost their humanity in the process. Some contemporary commentary, by contrast, identified the pauper population as potential recruits to the dangerous classes. So far from an inert mass, paupers were thought to constitute an active force that was easily mobilized against industry, order, property and propriety [165]. What are we to make of all of this? Were paupers so downtrodden as to be incapable of any resistance to the workhouse system, or did they find the resources to retain a sense of personal identity? Direct documentation to supply an authentic pauper perspective on these issues has not as yet been located. Instead, we must look at authority relations in the workhouse and the place of the pauper within them. To this we now turn.

The workhouse was often a disorderly institution. Its officers were exposed to a good deal of verbal abuse and sometimes to physical danger. Inmates, too, were at risk. Black eyes and other, allegedly self-inflicted, bodily damage incurred during exchanges with staff, were not perhaps uncommon [1, PRO/MH12/6845, James Bates, 13 July 1847]. Each institution also had its portion of rough tough elements who beat and bullied fellow paupers either for sport or to secure extra food and tobacco. Older men in particular were at the mercy of younger and stronger inmates whose respect for age or property were minimal [17]. Men, though, had no monopoly on disorder. The able-bodied women's wards were noted for their noise and disruption. Rowdiness and riotous conduct with violent assaults upon matron and her staff were by no means unknown. Collective violence, organized or spontaneous, was from time to time directed against unpopular officers, as at Liverpool in 1866, or in support of an individual inmate who had been wronged by the authorities. Kensington workhouse women's ward, for example, was the scene of one such disturbance in the late 1880s when the punishment of a refractory inmate provoked pandemonium: 'forty women rose to the rescue, assaulted the officers and barricaded the ward. The police were called in and they had to break the door open and carry four of the girls to jail' [134 *p. 162*].

Problems of workhouse discipline arose from the shifting nature of the inmate population and the fact that the pauper, unlike the convict, was not held under lock and key. Inmates were free to come and go as they pleased. Three hours' notice was all that was required to secure the release of the pauper and his family and the return of their clothes. The master of the workhouse had no power of detention and no right to refuse readmission. Workhouse order could not be taken for granted; its acquisition called for considerable management skill on the part of the master and his staff, particularly in the use of incentives and deprivations. Available to them was a vast repertoire of rewards and punishments. Diets were reduced and privileges rescinded, reprimands issued and punitive measures introduced. Troublemakers might be placed on bread and water for forty-eight hours. The master also possessed summary power to confine turbulent types in a separate room or cell for up to twenty-four hours. Those who gave satisfaction, by contrast, might be elevated to become servants or clerks to the master and receive pocket money or extra rations. Practices of this sort, though of dubious legality, were none the less effective for that. From such means arose a pauper pecking order that was sustained by a fine discrimination in the allocation of food and comforts and by preferential treatment in access to recreation and the use of tobacco. Exceptional provision was sometimes made for disorderly elements. Special refractory wards with barred windows and lockable doors were thus reserved for the seasonally unemployed who entered the workhouse in Liverpool and Lambeth during the turbulent initiatory phase of the New Poor Law. The sanctions of the criminal law were also available. Masters frequently required magistrates to uphold workhouse discipline. Paupers committed to gaol accounted for a fair proportion of petty offenders who appeared before magistrates throughout our period [25, 17].

Resort to the criminal law advertized the weakness of the poor law authorities but was unavoidable so long as the legislature remained deaf to their appeals for greater powers of command and control. This was generally considered impolitic. Parliament was at length persuaded to take action against an away-day element whose assertiveness and volatility were unseemly and subversive. The problem centred on capricious discharges and the disruption caused by able-bodied 'ins and outs' who quit the workhouse only to return after a twenty-four hour binge. The Pauper Inmates Discharge and Regulation Act of 1871 gave guardians power to limit the number of times a pauper could leave the workhouse in a week while the Poor Law Act of 1899 provided for the compulsory detention for one week of a pauper who was deemed by the guardians to have discharged himself frequently without sufficient reason. Neither measure proved an effective sanction; while powers for the removal of children, which were increasingly available to discipline recalcitrant parents, were too expensive to use.

Disorders varied from the full-scale riot to the use of foul language. Collective acts of indiscipline, prevalent in the 1830s and 1840s, were provoked by changes in the day-to-day management of the workhouse, in a tightening of work supervision or suspension of established leave arrangements, in measures which departed from routine and custom and seemed oppressive. A master, surcharged for the improper use of beer as a work incentive, was thus able to persuade the auditor that 'difficulties' would arise if the allowance was not restored [24 *p. 247*]. Acts of indiscipline became less dramatic as the century wore on. Individual rather than group action was the predominant form. Insubordination was thought to be rife among vagrants who misbehaved in order to be sent to prison where the food was better and officialdom no worse. True or not, offences committed by vagrants kept the magistrates' courts busy in the generation before the First World War.

It seems clear from the extent of indiscipline that inmates were neither silent nor submissive sorts who just did as they were told. Order was not simply a matter of imposition. Masters and matrons found it necessary to acquire appropriate manipulative skills to regulate and control their charges. By such means resistance was contained but never overcome. Contemporaries often found it convenient to dismiss insubordination, drunk and disorderly conduct or the destruction of workhouse property as meaningless acts of defiance and depravity. Other interpretations are possible. Modern historians have now acquired sufficient information on the conduct of individuals in total institutions – e.g., army, concentration camps, prisons and asylums – to consider inmate antagonism not as a form of mindless opposition but as the expression of individual and collective identities, the analysis of which is necessary for a proper understanding of how the system worked.

THE WORKHOUSE AND THE WORKING CLASS

'The Poor Law of 1834', writes one historian, 'came perhaps nearer than any other Act of Parliament in the nineteenth century to provoking a civil war in Britain' [149 *p. 151*]. Contemporaries were certainly alarmed by the depth of popular opposition that it provoked. Its introduction in the winter of 1834–35 initiated a decade of agitation and unrest in the southern and eastern counties, in the textile manufacturing districts and in rural Wales. Soldiers and policemen were required to oversee its enforcement. Villagers rose to secure the return of their poor from union workhouses or to prevent their removal from the parish. To them the New Poor Law appeared not only as an affront to customary relief practices but as a challenge to their very right to existence. Labourers gathered to demonstrate outside the new workhouses and vent their fears against an allegedly Malthusian regime that separated families to limit population, or tampered with workhouse food so as to reduce fertility. Such fears were sustained by an army of propagandists like the anonymous author of *Marcus on Populousness*, a spoof, written in the form of a report by a poor law commissioner, that pressed the case for infanticide as a solution to overpopulation and made plausible the rumoured arrival of an educational inspector in South Wales in 1839 whose brief was to prepare a census of children for extinction [25]. Emotions ran high. Disorders in the West Country resulted in the temporary postponement of the building of the Camelford workhouse. Rural incendiarism in East Anglia and Bedfordshire in 1844 was associated with opposition to the New Poor Law [52, 104]. Popular resistance in the industrial north was so fierce that the introduction of the New Poor Law was delayed until the 1860s [56, 65, 66, 67]. The anti-poor law movement, however, could check but not prevent the eventual triumph of the reformers. The New Poor Law thus became a fact which the labouring population could not ignore.

Pauperism was a form of degradation and disgrace. To apply for relief was a cause for self-reproach and private humiliation; to enter the workhouse was a public admission of personal and moral failure. The authorities did everything to make it so. The poor law system, with its workhouse and deterrent regime, was designed to impress upon the labouring population that economic security was an individual obligation in the natural order of the economic market. Thus it was the pauper and not the poor man who was deprived of rights of citizenship. The effect though, is uncertain. Popular responses towards the workhouse were not a simple reflection of approved values. There was in fact considerable variation which depended upon local circumstances, upon traditions of poor law administration and relief strategies, upon conditions in particular workhouses and upon the relative situation of labourers and paupers. Poor relief in the north east, for example, did not carry the sense of shame that was common in other regions where the poor would suffer any hardship to avoid entering the workhouse. Among the immigrant Irish of the 1840s it was the fear of removal under the settlement laws rather than the dread of a deterrent Poor Law that kept them off the relief rolls [99, 155]. For large numbers of the casual poor, though, the workhouse was a short-term resource to tide them over the emergencies that were a routine feature of their lives. Children from such backgrounds were thus admitted to the workhouse as a form of respite relief to enable a family in difficulties to resolve its problems [131, 146]. These, the marginal elements in the labour market who were unable to earn a steady living by regular work, relied upon the Poor Law as a matter of course as did beggars, vagabonds and others of the disreputable classes. The differences between them were not easily separable. Crime and poverty were not unrelated. Nor could the poor discard beggary, refuse charity or regard either as shameful.

The situation of the poorest elements within the working class was altogether more ambiguous than either the Victorian middle classes or modern historians have allowed. Insufficient attention has been devoted to life cycle poverty and the shifting importance of public and charitable assistance within working-class families. Those who sought assistance from the Poor Law did not in consequence become isolated from their community. Their absence was temporary: they were not shunned and relatives did not cease to see them in the workhouse. East End prostitute Frances Coles, for example, regularly visited her inmate father before her throat was cut in a Jack-the-Ripper-style attack in 1891. The poor man, brought out of the workhouse to identify his daughter's corpse, was not otherwise exceptional [2]. Relatives not only wanted to retain contact, but were capable of making the very devil of a row when visiting hours were restricted [61 *p. 223*]. Inmates and those denied assistance could be no less vociferous. Some, like Jeremiah Dunn [*Doc. 4*], made their requests in person; others acted collectively as did the Manchester paupers who sent a deputation to protest against the inadequate scale of family income supplements in 1848 [23 *p. 142*]. Many put pen to paper [72]. Their complaints, submitted to the central authority, suggest that they did not possess a self-image as disfranchised submerged sorts. Identities varied. 'A Mother' with difficulty cobbled together a couple of lines on behalf of her distressed children [*Doc. 7*]. Protesting paupers who presented themselves as 'we the undersigned petitioners' went on to itemize those aspects of the workhouse regime which violated their liberties and curtailed their rights as free-born Englishmen [1, PRO/MH12/7928, Petition of Richard Ogden *et. al* 11 February 1867]. The safety of anonymity was preferred by a scribe in the Whitechapel workhouse who prudently projected himself as 'One of the Victims' [*Doc. 12*]. The form of their communications as well as the substance of their complaints does not suggest that these correspondents regarded themselves as a class removed from civil society [*Docs. 5* and *8*]. Paupers, though often perceived as social outcasts, were not cut off from intercourse with the wider world. The lodging of complaints in writing constitutes an act of cultural and political participation which implies, among other things, that plaintiffs possessed a picture of the social and political order and of their situation within it. That situation, however, was not static.

As living standards rose at the close of the nineteenth century the gap between the peripheral poor and the respectable working class became wider. The workhouse loomed larger than previously in the imagination of the newly affluent artisan with pauperism and loss of independence becoming the penultimate form of social descent, exceeded only by imprisonment. The prospect of a pauper's funeral, however, made all respectable folk shudder. To be buried in an unmarked grave without ceremony, expense or dignity was an assault on personal identity and an affront to the most cherished values of class and community. Trade unionists as upholders of those values were particularly hostile to a Poor Law that seemed designed to depress wages and subvert labour organization. Guardians in cahoots with employers sometimes adjusted relief practices to sustain low wages or supplied blacklegs to undermine strike action. Guardians, who frequently were employers, also sought to discriminate against striking workers by means of exceptional severity in relieving distress with the denial of relief to those deemed to have made themselves unemployed. In this they were supported by the Court of Appeal which ruled in 1900 that guardians could not legally relieve an able-bodied man who could obtain work. Although the judgment also determined that the striking man's dependents were eligible for assistance, it did little to alleviate the sense of class bitterness which the Poor Law aroused. Poor Law involvement in initiatives such as the promotion of labour exchanges were considered suspect and cold-shouldered by trade unionists [25]. Work-based sources of hostility combined with the social stigma arising from contact with the poor law service exerted a significant influence upon the long-term development of social policy. The process of specialization notwithstanding, no popular support was available except for a national system of social assistance that was based on a repudiation of poor law principles. The welfare state was a negation rather than a continuation of the vision of 1834.

4 THE POOR LAW IN SCOTLAND

Poor relief in Scotland differed significantly from that in England and Wales. Under the Act of Union of 1707 Scotland retained its own legal and administrative systems. Separate legislation was required to reorganize relief arrangements in Scotland, and no such measure was brought forward until 1845, eleven years after the introduction of the New Poor Law in England and Wales. In England the able-bodied poor had a statutory right to relief. Poor relief in Scotland conceded no comparable right to assistance. Provision for the Scottish poor came not from local taxation, as in England and Wales, but from voluntary contributions under the management of the minister and his elders in the kirk session. English reformers of the 1830s were mightily impressed with the character-forming potential of the Scottish system compared with the pauperizing tendencies of the extravagant rate-supported system south of the border. Scottish reformers were proud to emphasize the contrast between a self-operating charitable system which strengthened the chain of sympathy between the classes and the baneful influence of a statutory Poor Law. Thomas Chalmers (1780–1847), the most famous of these reformers, achieved renown as the exponent of a 'natural' system of voluntary assistance in St John's, Glasgow in the early 1820s. Chalmers divided his parish into a number of small districts. Each district was placed in the care of a deacon of the church whose duty it was to visit and get to know the poor families of his district. Chalmers instructed his deacons that in cases of need they should first attempt to organize the resources of the family and its wider kin. Charitable aid should be only a second line of defence, with public relief as the very last resort [76]. His ideas, developed in *The Christian and Civic Economy of Large Towns* (1823), became a seminal text for those who believed that the abolition of a legal right to relief would prove equally beneficial in England and Wales.

Historians have in recent years begun to query the account as given above [84]. The contrast between organized voluntary relief as applied in Scotland and the tax-funded system in England and Wales has been overdrawn. The Scottish model which so appealed to the English reformers of the 1830s, it is now argued, was an imagined alternative rather than an accurate representation of Scottish relief practices. Scottish poor law legislation of the sixteenth and seventeenth centuries provides evidence of the recognition of a right to relief, supported, if need be, by compulsory assessments. Convergence with the English pattern which accelerated after the great famine of the 1690s was checked around the mid-eighteenth century after a number of legal decisions removed control over the Poor Law from the local inhabitants (assembled in the kirk sessions) to the principal ratepayers, the great landowners, who had every interest in resisting further movement towards the more generous system of poor relief south of the border. Their ability to do so also owed something to the nature of rural society in Scotland where population pressure and social structure were less demanding upon the provision of poor relief. Scottish agriculture, being more dependent upon subsistence cultivation and less commercialized than its English compeer, also carried less in the way of social costs. Important, too, was the organization of the labour force, and above all the reliance upon a regular married workforce hired annually, which obviated the need for Speenhamland-style wage subsidies. At the same time the exclusion of the able-bodied poor from relief facilitated the consolidation of larger estates without the build up of a surplus population as in the English southern counties. The need for a New Poor Law, then, was more pressing in England than in Scotland where canny landowners had secured control over local taxation by 1752 and arranged things – even to the extent of introducing English-style settlement laws – so as to minimize the burden of tax-funded social support [81, 83].

THE SCOTTISH POOR LAW AMENDMENT ACT, 1845

Industrialization, though it came later in Scotland, intensified social problems in a manner that was already familiar in England and Wales. The scale of unemployment in the towns and industrial districts, particularly during the manufacturing distress of 1839–42, exposed the deficiencies in voluntary relief practices and, as in England, fed fears of vagrancy and social disruption. The need for poor law reform, if not already irresistible, became unavoidable with the Disruption in the kirk in 1843. Apart from the attendant religious and social convulsions, the split in the Church of Scotland and the formation of a secessionist Free Church threw the kirk-based relief system into turmoil [77]. The Royal Commission appointed to inquire and suggest improvements undertook its duties with great celerity. Its report, issued in 1844, was comprehensive in scope and cogent in presentation. Nearly 100 per cent of Scottish parishes submitted returns which, with supporting evidence, amounted to seven volumes of some 15,000 pages. It concluded that resources were insufficient in relation to the demand for poor relief, that scales of relief were inadequate and the delivery system in need of reorganization. The report recommended the creation of a more efficient administrative structure with greater scope for the introduction of tax- supported poor relief [78, 80].

The Poor Law Amendment Act of 1845, which embodied the recommendations of the Royal Commission, created the administrative framework through which improved relief was given. It provided for the appointment of a Board of Supervision as the central authority to oversee and guide the newly-created parochial boards which were to be appointed annually in each parish to administer the poor fund. No provision was made for the compulsory levying of rates which was included as an optional extra. All that was required was that money should be available to provide regular adequate allowance to the poor. How that money was raised was a matter for local decision. Poorhouse provision, too, was left to local discretion as was the definition of those eligible for assistance. Whether the able-bodied unemployed received relief depended upon the generosity of the local authorities. There was no statutory right to relieve such persons. The temporary assistance granted by some parochial boards was, moreover, prohibited by a decision of the courts in 1859 which confined the definition of a pauper to those who were disabled and destitute. The Act of 1845 also included provisions for the feeble-minded, the education of pauper children and for medical assistance within and outwith the poorhouse.

The Edinburgh-based Board of Supervision was made up of nine members, drawn from the political and administrative-judicial elite, who were broadly representative of agrarian, industrial and urban interests. Its role was to advise and assist the organization of parochial boards in each of the 880 parishes in Scotland. The Board established its authority by stealth rather than through the imposition of its will upon the localities. Underresourced and without powers of compulsion or audit, it had no choice but to proceed with care in matters concerning the raising of funds and distribution of poor relief [78].

Investigation of the large number of complaints received from the public at large as well as from paupers led to a more interventionist stance. Rules and regulations, issued in response to such complaints, advised parishes on the prevention of abuse and upon improved methods in social administration. The Board's interventions, moreover, were by no means ineffective. Its determination to secure more adequate standards of relief was reflected in the increase in poor law expenditure after 1845. In order to comply with the Board's regulations for minimum standards of care and maintenance, parishes were forced to abandon their reliance upon voluntary contributions in favour of rate-supported relief. In 1894, 95 per cent of Scottish parishes levied a regular yearly rate compared with 25 per cent who did so in 1845.

The parochial boards, established under the Act of 1845, were appointed annually in each parish and were required to appoint an inspector as executive officer who acted as mediator with the Board of Supervision. Untrained and unqualified, most were lowly clerks for whom the post was a secondary form of employment. Their status and competence was gradually raised by the unremitting pressure of the Board of Supervision whose own powers of inspection were enhanced by special legislation in 1856. In the main, however, the Board made no attempt to secure uniformity in standards of provision. To the Inspector of the Poor fell the duty of deciding who was entitled to relief as well as the nature and duration of the assistance offered. There was no single determinant: parish resources, individual circumstances, local traditions – all affected relief practices. Apart from ensuring that an applicant did not die for want of assistance, the inspector could do pretty well as he pleased.

RECEPTION OF NEW SCOTTISH POOR LAW

Implementation of the Scottish Poor Law gave rise to no popular oppositional movement as in England and Wales. The reasons for this are fourfold. In the first place, Scottish poor law reformers found satisfaction in the courts rather than through legislation. As Rosalind Mitchison has shown Scottish Whigs had effectively rewritten the nation's legal textbooks before 1834 in order to achieve greater stringency in poor relief administration [82]. In the second place, there was greater continuity between the reformed and unreformed Poor Law than in England. Central-local tensions were much abated by the more gentle pace of local reorganization. In Scotland, administrative reform was accomplished without the creation of poor law unions and without the resistance to centralization and loss of identity which these forced boundary changes provoked. In the third place, controversy over rating was avoided by the simple expedient of including an optional rating clause in the legislation of 1845. Each parish, though required to furnish funds for adequate provision for the poor, was left to decide whether to raise rates for this purpose and whether to base assessments upon the rateable value of property or on personal income. Finally, and perhaps most important of all, there was no Chadwick figure armed with a blueprint for the reformation of Scottish society. Deterrence formed no part of the Scottish Poor Law. There was no attempt to abolish outdoor relief and in consequence no change in status of the Scottish workhouse which remained a home for the aged and disabled rather than an instrument for the repression of the able-bodied unemployed. The exclusion of the Scottish unemployed from a legal right to relief meant that a comparable situation could not, in any case, arise [79]. There was no question of providing organized employment in Scottish poorhouses and rather less controversy in consequence [85].

RELIEF PRACTICES

Outdoor relief was much preferred by parochial boards on grounds of economy and effort. Allowances were distributed in cash or in kind, although the two were often apportioned simultaneously. Weekly cash payments might be enhanced by diverse supplements. These embraced provision of clothing, bedding and fuel and payments of rents and rates. Medical aid and special food supplements for the sick were also available [75]. Those requiring further care could receive assistance as in-patients in poorhouse wards or in voluntary hospitals. Schooling for pauper and dependent children was also included. Child care relief was granted only after all matters of family support had been exhausted and intensive searches made for irresponsible parents. Scots practice in this respect differed markedly from that sanctioned by the poor-law authorities in England and Wales. Boarding-out pauper children to suitable guardians was deemed superior to institutional provision; it gave the disadvantaged child the benefits of a secure home, mainstream schooling, the prospect of a job and a chance to escape the influence of a degenerate environment and so break the cycle of dependency [92].

The quantity and quality of poor relief and the balance between indoor and outdoor assistance was left largely to local decision. The wisdom of these arrangements came to be questioned in the second half of the nineteenth century. The 'poorhouse test', recommended by the Board of Supervision in 1850, set the tone for a more forceful approach to the reduction of waste and extravagance. Laxity and mismanagement in respect of unsupervised outdoor relief became the target of reformers who were provoked by the resurgence of pauperism. This reached an all time high in 1868 when one in every twenty-four of the total population was a pauper. Moreover, out of a pauper host of 136,444 only 8,794 were inmates of poorhouses. Pressure to exercise greater discrimination in the use of outrelief began to be exerted by the Board of Supervision which also tried to encourage the more extensive use of indoor relief in order to deter frivolous applicants. The larger urban parishes, with their cadres of well-trained inspectors and assistant inspectors who knew how to coerce prodigal paupers into the poorhouse and how to persuade pauper parents to part with their children, were upheld as examples for other parochial boards to follow. Most lacked the resources to act on these lines. Nevertheless, there was an attempt to be more rigorous in the classification and differential treatment of the poor in order to increase discipline and control, to restrict outdoor relief to the 'deserving' poor and present the poorhouse as the abode of the socially inferior and morally deficient portion of the population. The transfer of the undeserving elements from outrelief to indoor relief would, it was hoped, act as a workhouse test. Relief rolls would then diminish on the assumption that recipients of outrelief, when confronted with loss of liberty, would prefer to shift for themselves and abandon claims for public assistance.

Pauperism certainly fell in late-nineteenth-century Scotland. By 1894 statistics compiled by the Board of Supervision showed that there was one pauper for every forty-four of the total population, that 91,212 were inmates of poorhouses and 72,891 paupers were in receipt of outdoor relief. No causal relation, though, has been established between these figures and the squeeze on outdoor relief of preceding years. Imperfections in the statistical data, one authority warns us, makes it unwise to draw any firm conclusions [85 *pp. 190–1*]. All we can say with confidence is that, like their counterparts in England and Wales, pauper inmates in Scottish poorhouses were hounded from pillar to post as the queen's reign drew to a close.

THE SCOTTISH POORHOUSE

Rules and regulations for the construction and management of poorhouses were issued by the central authority. Although the Scottish poorhouse was not assigned the same strategic function as the work-house in English poor law policy, the Board of Supervision and its successor the Scottish Local Government Board were just as con-cerned to ensure that accommodation was equal to the demand and of a suitable standard. Both aims were realized. Poorhouses more than doubled in number – from twenty-one to fifty – between 1850 and 1868. Old buildings, too, were refurbished and their facilities improved. By 1894 there were sixty-six poorhouses with accom-modation for more than 15,000 paupers and the staff to provide the specialized care that different categories of inmate required. As in the English workhouse, space was allocated to males and females, young and old, respectable and dissolute and to the sick.

The new buildings, many of them with central heating and sanita-tion far in advance of that to be found in the homes of the poor, were nevertheless underused. Although ample accommodation was avail-able, the average number of inmates was between 8,000 and 9,000 per year. Preference for outdoor relief remained strong among economy-minded administrators and traditionally-minded recipients who, for reasons of expense or convenience, valued care in the community above supervised provision in a poorhouse. As pauperism increased and costs rose, however, there was growing concern as to whether Scottish ratepayers could proceed without the introduction of at least an element of deterrence into relief practices. The attempt to do so did nothing to improve relations between inmates and staff in the poorhouse.

In respect of poorhouse management, parochial boards took their lead from the strict regime enforced by the Edinburgh authorities. Even so, it was quickly discovered that order could not simply be im-posed. Incentive schemes were required to secure a measure of consent for the discipline and control that were deemed necessary for the provision of supervised care. Approved conduct and inmate co-operation in undertaking routine tasks around the poorhouse earned extra amenities. Shoemaking, tailoring and internal maintenance work was offered to men; domestic duties were available to women. The poorhouse, though, was not a workhouse and there was no scope for the laborious and punishing work practices that were en-forced upon pauper inmates in England and Wales. Whether the alleged idleness of the Scottish pauper was a conscious form of resist-ance to poorhouse management remains to be established. As in England and Wales, the Scottish authorities had few powers of com-pulsion. Difficult inmates could not be detained against their will. Nor could they be denied relief. The most that could be done was to transfer such persons to outdoor relief, a policy which conflicted with the growing pressure from the central authority for tighter administration by means of a modified workhouse test.

Inmates, though, were not the only difficulty. Paupers on outrelief could be no less troublesome. The poor of urban Scotland were in fact a remarkably litigious lot. Many were familiar with legal procedures and quite adept at exploiting them in their everyday struggles over house tenure. Such knowledge was not based on book-learning. Contact with the Poor Law is the more likely source. The Scottish system differed from the English system in that the destitute possessed a right of appeal against the denial of relief, against inadequate relief and against mistreatment in the poorhouse. The Poor Law Amendment Act of 1845 encouraged paupers to assert their right to adequate care and provided free legal aid to pursue the claim where the central authority determined that a just cause for court action had been established [25]. Those with grievances were entitled to complain in writing to the Board of Supervision, and between 1845 and 1894, 20,000 allegations of inadequate relief were received. More than half these claims were rejected. However, one in five cases was sent back to the relevant parochial board with recommendations for remedial action [85]. The system, then, was designed to deter all but the most resolute of paupers and in this, it no doubt succeeded. For the persistent, however, participation in the legal process could be advantageous. Scottish tenants found it so [112].

CONCLUSION

The Scottish Poor Law differed significantly from that of England and Wales. The organizing assumptions of the legislation of 1845 were far less radical than those of Chadwick and his associates on the Royal Commission of 1832–34. The pace of change was slower, attitudes towards the poor more stable and continuity in poor relief practices pronounced. Scottish paupers, though, were no less marginal and no less deprived than their compeers in England and Wales. Their misery, moreover, was not much diminished by the administrative changes that took place around them. The steady movement towards a more centralized system accelerated after 1894. In that year the Scottish Local Government Board took over from the Board of Supervision as the central authority. Armed with powers of audit, it was better placed than its predecessor to control the elected parish councils that replaced the old parochial boards. Similarities with English poor law policy, thereafter, became marked even to the extent of a Majority/Minority split on the Scottish Poor Law Commission of 1905–9 comparable with that on its English-Welsh counterpart. The Scottish Minority Report, drafted by the Webbs, includes the finest statement of their social vision [25].

5 SOCIAL INQUIRY AND POOR LAW REFORM

POVERTY AND PAUPERISM

'While the problem of 1834 was the problem of pauperism, the problem of 1893 is the problem of poverty'. Alfred Marshall's much-quoted statement to the Royal Commission on the Aged Poor signalled the shift that had allegedly taken place in contemporary thinking about social problems. The nature of that shift and how it came about, though, remains unclear. It is sometimes presented as a movement from individualism to collectivism.* This is misleading [148]. Among the most enthusiastic exponents of social reform were many who rejected collectivism. Among those identified as collectivists were some who were pronounced anti-socialists. The heightened awareness of social problems that made the 1880s an apparent turning-point in the development of social policy had various sources. Evolutionary thinking underscored the importance of impersonal social forces. It focused upon social organization and tended to discount the free choices of rational individuals that had been emphasized by political economy. Society constituted a living organism. National well-being depended upon its ability to respond to external social change. Positive action was required to combat conditions that threatened the health and vitality of the commonweal [103]. Influential, too, were the Oxbridge Idealists gathered around Arnold Toynbee (1852–1883) and T. H. Green (1836–1882). Idealism,* as expounded by them, derived from German metaphysics a concept of citizenship which assumed the existence of a good common to all classes that could be expressed in concrete measures of social improvement. Idealists were moralists for whom the purpose of human existence was the pursuit of the common good rather than the satisfaction of private wants. The cadre of socially aware activists who were inspired by Green and his teachings came to occupy key positions in the network of societies and institutions which kept the public abreast of social questions [160]. It is not helpful to pidgeon-

hole organicists like Charles Booth (1840–1916) and Seebohm Rowntree (1871–1954) or their Idealist critics in the Charity Organization
Society as either individualists or collectivists. The issues which separated them concerned the forms of social protection and the balance
between public and private provision in the organization of welfare.

The place of social inquiry in all of this also has a bearing upon the
movement of ideas. Orthodox economic theories and the social
policies such theories justified had been called into question by
changes in the intellectual and material environment. The idea that
poverty was a natural condition and pauperism a matter of choice
had been shaken by the crisis in political economy. The destruction of
the wage-fund theory and the declining importance attached to excessive population pressure undermined confidence both in the utility
and integrity of political economy. Its conception as a set of mechan-
ical laws that were independent of morality and capable of revealing
an ordered reality drew criticism from several quarters. Some argued
that the deductive method of classical economics* simplified and dis-
torted reality; others sought to recast the science of wealth as the
science of welfare and create a new economics devoted to individual
and social regeneration. To such critics, the gloomy projection of a
future based on increasing scarcity seemed out of step with the possibilities of working-class improvement opened up by industrial and
technological development. The reconstruction of social theory, a
process that had begun in the 1870s, became pressing during the
1880s as the onset of economic depression, mass unemployment, an
extended franchise and social unrest, exposed the deficiencies in orthodox economics. Charles Booth's path-breaking survey *Life and
Labour of the People in London* should be seen in relation to the
search for an economic theory that was less abstract, less deductive
and rather more serviceable than that of the classical school [144].

TRADITIONS OF SOCIAL INQUIRY

Life and Labour of the People in London provided the first scientific
estimates of poverty and has been regarded as the starting-point of all
serious discussion of the subject ever since. To the line of pauperism
separating the self-supporting from the dependent elements of the
population, Booth added a line of poverty beneath which subsisted a
third of the population who lacked an income sufficient for family
maintenance at the accepted standard of working-class comfort. *Life
and Labour of the People in London* did not emerge from nowhere
but was the high point in a tradition of social inquiry that had its

origins in the social emergency created by the Industrial Revolution. Industrialization disturbed and disrupted the social fabric. It led to migration from the countryside and the growth of towns; it changed family roles and relationships [143] and made people dependent upon paid employment for their livelihood; it called forth new forms of industrial discipline and new forms of social control. Contemporaries were at once pleased and provoked by the unprecedented nature of the industrial transformation. Urbanization, in particular, gave cause for concern. The concentration of propertyless masses in large towns and populous districts from which the rich had fled, left the poor without proper guidance and deprived of the sympathy and benevolence that were considered critical to the reproduction of deference and maintenance of the social order. Social investigation in Britain was firmly grounded in these fears. The sense of social crisis which gave it its momentum also explains the narrowing conception of its field of activity. Social investigation fixed its eyes firmly on the study of the present, upon things as they are rather than on how they came to be. The various bodies that undertook the work, official and private, were primarily fact-gathering agencies. Information was required to publicize discrete social evils and promote remedial action. Social investigation, as the Victorians understood it, was not concerned to generate general theories of social development, nor was it engaged in as an intellectual exercise. Particularist and piecemeal in scope and approach, it was undertaken largely as a guide to social action.

It was this demand for information which, from the 1830s onwards, prompted the appointment of the great royal commissions and select committees of inquiry and the establishment of local statistical societies. These brought together interested parties from industry, philanthropy and public service who engaged in social research and, by means of conferences, and contributions to press and periodical publications, created a network for the exchange of ideas and diffusion of research skills and techniques. They also engaged in a constructive dialogue with the registrar-general, the nascent factory and poor law inspectorates and with those involved in official inquiries. Curious and creative, they made interesting innovations in survey methods in social investigation – in questionnaire design, sampling techniques and reporting procedures – and developed promising theoretical perspectives on, for example, the possibilities of family budget analysis. Most of the statistical societies, however, were unstable bodies whose achievements and possibilities were soon forgotten. The more robust London (subsequently Royal) Statistical

Society survived to play an important part as a network for the exchange of ideas and research skills. It also inspired the formation of the National Association for the Promotion of Social Science, the single most important pressure group of its kind [113].

The Social Science Association, as the NAPSS was popularly known, was formed in 1857. Social issues of every kind received an airing on its platforms and in its publications. It has been presented by some historians as the think-tank of Gladstonian Liberalism. But it was more than that. The Association differed from predecessor organizations in its critical approach to social theory and in the active support of women's participation. The poor were held to be women's special concern and space sought for appropriate action. The Poor Law as the very embodiment of predatory individualist political economy was in particular need of attention. The Workhouse Visiting Society, formed by Lousia Twining* in 1858, thus received encouragement. It brought love and light to the indigent poor, and when that was not enough, turned to political action to secure improvement. The Society for Promoting the Return of Women as Poor Law Guardians, though, was not the only way in which poor law reform was carried forward. The Social Science Association itself sponsored annual conferences of Poor Law Guardians which in 1877 became the Central Committee of Poor Law Conferences. Pauperism, of course, loomed large in its thinking about the nature of social divisions and their implications for social action. Paupers along with the irregularly employed and semi-criminal elements were sharply distinguished from the authentic or self-supporting working class. Noteworthy, too, were its attempts to explain these distinctions by reference to the workings of the labour market and the organization of employment. The 'residuum' and its repression, once considered the centrepiece of the social strategies of the 1880s, is now recognized as less of an innovation than was previously imagined. Foreshadowed in Mayhew's depiction of social and cultural degeneration, it became an organizing concept of the mid-Victorian debate on the political integration of the working classes. Its condition figured prominently in the thinking of the Social Science Association. In its emphasis upon the importance of classification, the recognition accorded the underemployed and the unfit and the significance assigned to the overstocked London labour market, it anticipated much of Charles Booth's subsequent attempts to recast the social problem and make it amenable to administrative reform [120, 122, 165].

CHARLES BOOTH AND SOCIAL REFORM

Charles Booth was one of the foremost influences on social policy in the generation before the First World War. By the close of the nineteenth century he occupied a position comparable with that held by Chadwick at the time of the queen's accession. The two men, indeed, shared much in common. Both were committed to the civilizing mission of middle-class radicalism and both subscribed to the moral categories of Benthamite social analysis. Both had a preference for large-scale administrative solutions to social problems and both saw social inquiry as the basis for social action. Not surprisingly, both men have received nominations as the founder of the British school of empirical social research. There were, though, certain differences in personality. No one accused Booth of being overbearing or an impossible colleague. Those who knew him spoke highly of his skill, tact and general ability to set individuals at their ease and make them willing participants in his extraordinary investigations.

Charles James Booth was born in Liverpool into a public-spirited commercial family that was Liberal in politics and Unitarian in religion. Schooled at a unitarian academy, he completed his education at Apenzell in German-speaking Switzerland where the primacy of moral character and public service were exalted. Earnest, serious and civic-minded, he combined the development of his shipping line with an active commitment to franchise reform, popular education and social betterment. Booth, though, was no ordinary member of the privileged classes. Conventional Christianity held no appeal. Positivism,* the Religion of Humanity, presented a more satisfying foundation for a rational faith. Positive Philosophy offered the young, the intellectually curious and those of unsettled faith a humanist religion and a new ethic of social obligation. Booth was among them. Like so many of his generation he was repelled by the crass materialism of the age and the selfishness it encouraged. Competition, a benign force necessary to the development of human and material resources, was, he feared, becoming blind to all but the creation of wealth. Its abolition, he believed, was both impractical and undesirable. Restraint and redirection, on the other hand, were in the national interest. Competition, he wrote in 1870, 'now needs checking and that it is only in its subordination to public welfare that we can look for that social improvement which we need' [3, MS797/II/25/2]. The sectarianism that destroyed his attempt to introduce free secular education into Liverpool's schools convinced him that Humanity could be better served by means other than politics.

The social crisis of the 1880s gave a clear focus to his brooding intellect and expanding moral imagination.

By this time Booth had moved from Liverpool to London where family wealth and connections gave ready access to that band of moralists, philanthropists and members of the professional classes who dominated public debate on the social question. As a Positivist believing that social action should be grounded in the scientific study of the laws of society, Booth found himself both moved and fascinated by the lives of the working poor. The priority of east London in his thinking, however, derived not only from the scale of casual employment in that quarter. The influence of his wife Mary and her cousins – including the formidable Beatrice Potter – who were engaged in voluntary work in Whitechapel, also contributed to that quickening of interest which led Booth to take lodgings in the East End and invite workmen to his home in the West End in order to broaden his understanding of life and conditions in the greatest city in the world.

Economic recession, unemployment and political disturbance gave these interests a new urgency. Such anxieties as he possessed, however, found release in social inquiry rather than in social work. Impatient with the glacial pace of casework philanthropy, critical of the *a priori* assumptions of political economy and disturbed by the challenge of socialism, Booth gave primacy to the collection of facts and an accurate description of the conditions of the people as the basis for social diagnosis and public policy. The Life and Labour Inquiry was begun in 1886. The first volume of *Life and Labour of the People in London* was published in 1889, the seventeenth and final volume in 1903. In between, the work passed through several editions with much arrangement and rearrangement of chapters and contents. It was divided into three series – Poverty, Industry and Religious Influences. The first, which consisted of four volumes, was concerned with the definition and measurement of poverty and sought to relate degrees of well-being and comfort to the ways in which people lived. The second examined in five volumes how people worked, what they produced and what they received. The seven-volume third series, in spite of its title, was primarily concerned to set the distinctive and localized character of organized religion within the wider context of working-class culture. The whole project involved a large team of researchers who were supervised and financed by Booth himself in what was probably the largest private inquiry ever undertaken.

MAYHEW AND BOOTH COMPARED

Booth's was not the first investigation of conditions in the capital. Nearly forty years earlier the radical journalist Henry Mayhew (1812–1887) had conducted a similar inquiry. In 1849–50 Mayhew produced some eighty-two letters for the *Morning Chronicle*, about a million words in all, devoted primarily to the condition of the London manufacturing trades. In the next two years he published the equally weighty *London Labour and the London Poor*, an investigation in sixty-three weekly parts of the metropolitan street trades. A partially finished survey of the prison population, undertaken in 1855–56, was completed with outside assistance and published as *The Criminal Prisons of London* in 1862. All three inquiries were closely connected. Mayhew was identified by contemporaries as the founder of a new school of investigative journalism. The claim, even if exaggerated, does highlight the importance of a form of social inquiry which has not received the attention it deserves. Investigative journalism made a signal contribution to the mobilization of public concern on certain social problems. Prominent among them was the New Poor Law. The focus was less on policy and more on inmate experience as disclosed by eye-witness accounts or by means of personal inquiry and direct observation. Dickens' 'Wapping Workhouse', with its submissive and despondent inmates, seemed all the more moving for being cast as authentic empirical research. Equally authoritative – and for much the same reason – was the serialized and harrowing account of conditions in the Lambeth workhouse filed by James Greenwood, 'The Amateur Casual', who disguised himself to report his observations from the casual ward. Distinguished practitioners in the art of investigative journalism also included G. A. Sala (1828–1896) and George Sims* who, if now remembered at all, is best known for his poem 'In the Workhouse: Christmas Day'. Paupers in their environment were presented by this 'school of journalistic philanthropists', as a contemporary called them, in a way that was calculated to engage their readers' sympathies, disturb their equipoise and make the case for Poor Law reform suddenly seem urgent. Henry Mayhew might not have been the founder of this school, but there is no disputing his position as one of its greatest exponents [114, 129].

Mayhew made his way around the metropolis gathering personal testimonies from large numbers of artisans and labourers, street traders, prostitutes and distressed needlewomen, rag pickers, thieves, swindlers and others. Sensitive to the spoken word and with a novelist's eye for detail, Mayhew's first-person narratives provide support for his claim, made in the preface to *London Labour and the London Poor*, that his is the first book 'to publish the history of a people from the lips of the people themselves . . . in their own "unvarnished" language' [14 Vol. I]. Mayhew's mission, as he himself defined it, was to act as an intermediary between the classes, and to explain to one half how the other half lived. This led him from the assessment of the insufficiency of wages to an exploration of the changes in manufacturing activity associated with the expansion of the sweated trades to show how labour power had become a commodity organized and cheapened to suit the needs of its purchasers. Mayhew was equally interested in the outlook of his informants, with their traditions and memories, and the connection between their work and way of life. Torn between the competing claims of popular journalism and serious social inquiry, he nevertheless tried to show that behind the apparent chaos of their lives, there existed among his informants a pattern, structure and meaning with which his readers could understand and sympathize.

Mayhew's investigations were, in part, an expression of middle-class anxieties provoked by the narrow informational base of the Condition of England Question.* Mayhew, the wayward son of a prosperous London solicitor, shared much of the outlook and energy of the enlightened middle classes. He was a Fellow of the Royal Statistical Society, graced the platform of the Society for Promoting the Amendment of the Law and presented himself as an expert witness before parliamentary enquiries on social questions. He abhorred socialism, expressed reservations about trade unionism, supported emigration, and generally favoured profit-sharing arrangements. Persuaded by his findings of the deficiencies of population-based or market-led theories of poverty, he broke with political economy but remained close to the organizing assumptions of utilitarian radicalism particularly in his thinking about pauperism, crime and the dangerous classes.

The intellectual framework of the Mayhew Inquiry was rooted in middle-class concerns about the submergence of the labouring classes and their descent into the dangerous classes. Population growth and industrial change, it was feared, had disturbed the social order and created a race of vagabonds leading a nomadic existence without ties of family or community and with no respect for the rights of property. They were considered comparable to savages in the precariousness of their existence, impatience of labour and hatred of discipline. Atavistic fears about hordes of sturdy beggars roaming the country and despoiling people and property received a fresh focus from the growth of Chartism and cholera, prompting demands for a more repressive social policy. The spirit of the Tudors was much invoked by those who felt that the smack of firm government and close regulation were required to safeguard the realm and prevent the dangerous and disorderly elements from distracting and subverting the regular working class above them. Mayhew was among them. He reserved considerable space for the discussion of the life-style of criminals and beggars and chronicled their deceptions in great detail. He accepted the case for special action outside the Poor Law and found nothing objectionable in the suggestion that habitual vagrants should be placed under police supervision. Upon habitual criminals, i.e. confirmed vagabonds, he was even more severe. The 'primitive' classes, he argued, should be transported for life. The importance of education in the key initiatory stages was essential to the formation of habits of industry by which the social problem could be solved.

Mayhew's arguments about the insufficiency of earnings or his brilliant insights into the structure and organization of the casual labour market seemed rather less relevant to contemporaries than his observations on pauperism in relation to the dangerous classes. His attempt to trace poverty to the workings of the industrial system seems to have received far less attention that his exposure of roguish beggars, the mischievous effects of indiscriminate alms-giving and the need for a more effective repression of mendicity. It was this which made *London Labour and the London Poor* approved reading by the Charity Organization Society. Mayhew's unsympathetic approach to the undeserving poor was not dissimilar from that of Booth. The utilitarian cast of their analyses made for a continuity in outlook which contemporaries readily appreciated. Not for nothing was *Life and Labour of the People in London* regarded as the natural successor to *London Labour and the London Poor*. The Booth Inquiry, when first published, was viewed as a complement to and extension of the Mayhew survey [3, Press Cuttings].

Still, there were significant differences. The importance assigned to imperfections in the labour market was a distinctive feature in Booth's thinking. From the first his study of poverty centred on the situation of the worker in the labour market. The repudiation of Malthusian economics pointed him towards the possibilities of state intervention to relieve exceptional pressure in the metropolis. Booth's proposals for the decasualization of dock labour and support for non-contributory old age pensions together represented a coherent plan for the rationalization of the labour market and removal of the residual elements from it. Mayhew, though he too had broken with general theories of overpopulation, was unable to formulate a comparable strategy for social reform. Mayhew fixed upon the formation of the outcast poor, Booth upon its reduction.

POVERTY REDEFINED

Mayhew, though he readily grasped the possibilities of a poverty line, never provided an operational definition for its application. Booth not only supplied a basis for measurement and comparison, but also set out to separate those perceived as social problem groups from the self-supporting elements of the population and establish the relative size of each. For this purpose the population was divided into eight economic classes. Class A included 'the lowest class of occasional labourers, loafers and semi-criminals'; Class B, 'the very poor' living on casual earnings; while Classes C and D lived on intermittent and small regular earnings and together made up 'the poor'. Classes E and F, who subsisted above the line of poverty, constituted the authentic working class. The boundaries between classes were fluid and variable and difficult to distinguish, not least because Booth included non-material influences, like providence, thrift and sobriety, in an attempt to establish 'the prevailing type' in each class. 'By the word "poor",' he explained, 'I mean to describe those who have a sufficiently regular though bare income, such as 18 to 21 shillings per week for a moderate family, and by "very poor" those who from any cause fall below this standard. The poor are those whose means may be sufficient but are barely sufficient for decent independent life; the very poor are those whose means are insufficient for this according to the usual standard of life in this country. My "poor" may be described as living under a struggle to obtain the necessaries of life and make both ends meet, while the very poor live in a state of chronic want' [10, Poverty Series, Vol. 1 *p. 33*].

Booth proceeded to give full particulars to illustrate the types and conditions of the families he had in mind. The situation of Class B was critical. This class of casual labourers accounted for 11.25 per cent of the whole population and was deemed economically valueless and socially worthless. It was likened to a sump into which sank all the downwardly mobile elements of the labour force. The characteristics of this 'useless class' were easily recognized. Apart from a recessive restlessness, its members were described as shiftless, helpless, idle and drunken. Close to destitution, although not actually destitute, they were regarded as paupers-in-waiting whose destiny was already known. Class B, in short, was the social problem. 'Every other class can take care of itself, or could do so, if Class B were out of the way', wrote Booth. 'These unfortunate people form a sort of quagmire underlying the social structure, and to dry up this structure must be our principal aim' [10, Poverty Series, Vol. 1 *pp. 175–6*].

The classification of the population according to the degree of want or comfort in which they were found was not, however, based upon household income, which was not available, but on information acquired by the School Board Visitors* in the normal course of their duties. No house-to-house survey was undertaken. In Booth's own words the classification 'was based on opinion only – that is, on the impressions made on the minds of the School Board Visitors and others by what they had seen or heard as to the position in the scale of comfort of the people amongst whom they lived and worked' [10, Industry Series, Vol. 1 *p. 11*]. The opinions of the School Board Visitors were cross-checked against those of philanthropists, social workers, policemen and others. The scope for error was considerable. Booth's poverty line was controversial in his own day and has remained so ever since. Modern scholars wonder where on earth he got the idea from; contemporary critics wished he had never got it at all. Booth's line of poverty, it is suggested, was based on a relativistic concept of poverty borrowed from the London School Board. The poverty lines adopted by that body to define criteria of eligibility for the remission of school fees under the provisions of the Education Act of 1870 were used by Booth to define his own line of poverty [118]. The sources of the poverty line, however, are less important than the politics of the poverty line, which only became a contested concept once it was realized that it might provide the basis for an interventionist social policy designed to raise incomes. By that time *Life and Labour of the People in London* had reached its final edition. Seventeen years earlier, when unrest was rising, Booth's novel approach to the measurement of poverty was critical in relieving tension and restoring confidence among the propertied classes [63].

Booth's finding that 35 per cent of the population lived below the line of poverty was both surprising and reassuring. He had expected far worse. Contemporaries, too, were relieved. Attention fixed upon Booth's declaration that 65 per cent of the population were living in relative comfort and that the nightmarish vision of insurgent mobs marching westwards from Aldgate Pump, conjured by radicals like Henry George (1839–1897) and journalists like G. R. Sims, was without foundation. 'The handful of barbarians whom we have heard, who, issuing from their slums, will one day overwhelm modern civilisation, do not exist,' he wrote. 'There are barbarians, but they are a handful, a small and decreasing percentage: a disgrace but not a danger' [10, Poverty Series, Vol. I *p. 39*]. Booth was confident that remedial action was possible.

Booth's leading ideas took shape in the early 1880s. In these years, he abandoned the idea that attributed poverty to excessive population growth and began to consider the potentially liberating role of organization in the solution of the social problem. Socialist attempts to mobilize London labour and the London poor in the name of a unitary working class underscored the need for a counter strategy that would separate and rearrange the submerged and labouring classes so as to identify the basis for selective social action. The reconceptualization of the social problem in this way enabled him to advance a programme that, at once, promised not only to 'secure the final divorce of labour from poverty', but also to preserve property, promote independence and deprive socialism of a constituency [114 cf. 125].

It was the mode of employment which supplied the organizing insight for his reform programme. Booth, as a large employer of port labour, had a shrewd understanding of the imperfections in the labour market, and from the outset his classificatory scheme assumed a close correspondence between degrees of poverty and forms of work [122]. Posing the problem in these terms allowed him to advance the case for limited action to resist the downward pressure of the outcast poor upon those who might otherwise be incorporated into the working class proper. The removal from the labour market of the helpless, incompetent and unfit elements concentrated in Class B would, he argued, push Classes C and D upwards above the line of poverty into self-supporting habits. Booth, like most contemporaries, possessed a highly differentiated picture of the working classes. The key distinctions were between skilled and unskilled, rough and respectable, deserving and undeserving, between the practitioners of self help and mutual aid who tried to preserve an independent existence and the 'residuum' of casual workers, loafers, unemployables and ne'er-do-wells whose moral and physical degeneration threatened to pull down the self-supporting elements above them.

The prevention of such convergence supplied the impetus for a bold programme of social reform. Booth believed that special action was required to remove the very poor from paid employment and argued for coercive state action and 'an extension of the Poor Law' [10, Poverty Series, Vol. I *p. 165*], as the instrument for its realization. The possibility was considered that the inefficient elements of the population might be forcibly segregated into labour colonies, deprived of civil liberties and subject to stringent physical controls in order to safeguard the independent or respectable working class. The inmates of these colonies or industrial homes, as they were sometimes called, would be 'gradually absorbed into other industries, or, if the worst comes to the worst, they pass through the workhouse and finally die'. Booth had no doubt about the severity of his proposal. 'However slowly and kindly it may be done', he wrote, 'it is not a pleasant process to be improved off the face of the earth' [10, Poverty Series, Vol. I *pp. 163–70*]. Booth's subsequent advocacy of non-contributory old age pensions, a measure designed to liberate the 'true' working class from the competition of the aged poor, was simply a less repressive aspect of the same strategy.

PAUPERISM IN RELATION TO OLD AGE

The reorganization of the labour market, however, raised questions about the role and status of the Poor Law. The placement of the unfit under a form of 'state slavery' combined with the removal of the aged from the workhouse pointed to the inefficiency or irrelevance of the Poor Law and indicated the need for a review of relief practices and principles. For Booth this was a major preoccupation. *Life and Labour of the People in London* included a systematic survey of metropolitan poor law administration alongside detailed studies of poor law inmates while subsequent writings were specially directed at the relationship between pauperism and old age. To these we must now turn.

It is sometimes suggested that the Booth Inquiry was central in the transition from a conception of poverty based on individual failings to one which emphasized impersonal economic causes. This is too simplistic. Booth, having measured the extent of poverty, tried on several occasions to analyse its causes. First, he examined the circumstances of 4,000 of the poor and very poor families known to the School Board Visitors. Here the causes of poverty were arranged under the three heads: 'employment' which included lack of work and low pay; 'habit' which took in idleness, drink or thriftlessness, and 'circumstances' which covered sickness and large family. His finding that 55 per cent of the poverty of Classes A and B and 68 per cent of the poverty of Classes C and D were attributable to unemployment did not signify a shift to a radical conception of poverty based on involuntary causes. Quite the contrary. Incapacity for work leading to low pay and irregularity of employment, he declared, was very much a matter of individual weakness and personal inadequacy. 'There are those who never learn to do anything well on the one hand, and those who cannot get up in the morning on the other'. In brief, the unemployed and the incapacitated were readily interchangeable. 'The unemployed', he wrote, 'are as a class a selection of the unfit,' and added, 'on the whole, those most in want are the most unfit. This is the crux of the position'. The poor, he concluded, were the principal cause of their own poverty. 'To the rich the very poor are a sentimental interest; to the poor they are a crushing load. The poverty of the poor is mainly the result of the competition of the very poor' [10, Poverty Series, Vol. I *p. 154*].

Booth's willingness to embrace state action to eliminate that disruptive competition did not for one moment imply a rejection of the principles of 1834. Poverty, he believed, was a permanent condition which might be contained but not eradicated. Measures to remove the residual elements from the labour market to improve production and raise the value of labour did not, in his view, obviate the need for a deterrent Poor Law to prevent demoralization and dependency. At the core of Booth's thinking lay an unswerving belief not in the particular formulations of political economy but in the idea that individuals were motivated by the pleasure of idleness rather than the pain of industry (described in the literature as a hedonistic theory of psychological action) which made the abolition of the Poor Law unthinkable. Booth's study of the inmate population, which highlighted the need for pensions reform, also pinpointed the persistent failings of the unworthy and undeserving poor.

Booth's investigation into the causes of pauperism in three unions was first published in 1892 as *Pauperism and the Endowment of Old Age*. That part dealing with the Stepney Union was subsequently incorporated into the final edition of *Life and Labour of the People in London*. Booth's data, based on privileged access to the relieving officer's case books, confirmed the precarious condition of the labouring classes. His tabulations [*Doc. 15*] showed the ease with which the struggling poor became the destitute poor. Thus, in the Stepney Poor Law Union, old age was the 'principal cause' of poor law dependency in 33 per cent of cases and sickness was a principal cause in a further 27 per cent of cases. Incapacity (i.e. disability) and unemployment accounted for fifty-two cases, or 8 per cent of the whole, while death of the husband and wife-desertion accounted as principal causes for 4.6 per cent of indoor pauperism. Readers, although left in no doubt as to the necessity of special action for the aged poor, were also reminded of the continued relevance of a reformed Poor Law in the war against indigence. As with previous attempts to identify the apparent causes of poverty, the distinctions which Booth drew between the 'principal' and 'contributary' causes of pauperism reserved a significant role for non-economic influences. The connection between pauperism and the public house, for example, remained noteworthy. Drink stood as principal cause in 80 out of 634 cases, or 12.6 per cent, while drink and drink-related cases accounted for 25 per cent of the total, an estimate which Booth considered conservative. Then there was crime, immorality, laziness, temper, extravagance, restlessness and bad luck. Together with drink, these accounted for around 20 per cent of the principal causes of pauperism. The relative importance of these items, though, was not always easy to determine. Temper, for example, was bracketed with disability. Notions of heredity were likewise employed in a loose way. Booth, like many contemporaries, seems to have believed that pauperism ran in the family and was to some extent as much a biological as a social problem. 'Pauper association and heredity' while only accounting as a principal cause for seven cases was thus listed as a contributory cause in no less than one hundred and five cases.

Booth's tabulations, presented as an example of what could be done rather than as the basis for sound generalization, were supported with sixty-two case histories taken from the relieving officer's journals together with a digest of every case on the Stepney rolls for the twelve months up to April, 1887. The aim, Booth explained, was to provide a complete cross-section of indoor pauperism that would serve to illustrate the habits of the poor as well as the condition of pauperism. The difficulty here was that his classification was so flexible as to render distinctions meaningless. 'Incapacity and mental disease', he remarked, 'might be stretched to cover almost all – vice, drink, laziness, themselves closely bound together, fill also a great place in connection with sickness and lack of work – or we may reverse this, and show how sickness and lack of work, and consequent want of proper food, end in demoralisation of all kinds, and especially in drink' [10, Industry Series, Vol 4 *pp. 314–16*]. Booth's confidence in his 'rough-and-ready' method of analysis, though it infuriates modern scholars, was probably not misplaced. The picture of pauperism which he had drawn was sufficiently clear to support his preferred strategy of reform.

Booth's argument that old age pensions would serve to improve the efficiency of the Poor Law gained strength from a systematic study of the metropolitan poor law unions. The Booth Inquiry, it should be emphasized, was something more than a survey of poverty, work and wages. Booth was equally concerned with popular customs and habits, and with the values, beliefs and general outlook of the working population. Seven of the seventeen volumes of *Life and Labour of the People in London* were preoccupied with these aspects of the social question. Here, among other things, Booth tried to estimate the influence of locality upon the organization and shape of working-class culture. Chief among such influences was the character of poor law administration. The maintenance of public welfare in its widest sense was, he felt, closely connected with local management. The democratization of guardian elections in 1894 had transformed the Poor Law into a training school for the working classes. The quality of local leadership and tone of proceedings set a standard for good or ill in respect of self-maintenance and self-respect. Contemporaries feared that such standards would be found wanting, and that the abolition of the property qualification presaged waste, extravagance and a further weakening of morale. Booth, though confident that the rating system would moderate deviant and dangerous tendencies on the part of working-class representatives, was concerned about the variation in relief practices that existed. The impressions which he gathered seemed to suggest that while overall support for the principles of 1834 still held, commitment to deterrence was by no means universal [10, Religious Influences Series].

Booth, who broadly supported the strategy for a co-ordinated attack on outdoor relief as pursued by the Local Government Board since 1871, thought that greater unification among poor law unions and further measures of rate equalization would prevent backsliding among the poorer authorities and reinforce the campaign against demoralization. Booth, in fact, was much less hostile to the Charity Organization Society than they were to him. With much of their principles and practices he was in agreement, and he found much to admire in their social analysis. Indeed, he was pleased to recommend the Whitechapel COS as an exemplar of best practice in respect of public-private relief effort. Where they parted company was in respect of Booth's contention that pensions reform was the final stage in effective poor law reform.

Apart from the influence of local administration, the Booth Inquiry also noted the subversive effects of specialization within the Poor Law. The dissociation of medical services, in particular, had transformed the status of the workhouse infirmary. 'To go into the workhouse is considered a disgrace', said a Hackney informant, 'but the infirmary is regarded as a public hospital' [10, Religious Influences Series, Vol. 1 *p. 108*]. A similar softening was observed in relation to the treatment of ' the aged and deserving poor' who were increasingly separated from the inmate population and loaded with

privileges and comforts. Booth viewed this particular form of specialization as a socially benign development which, if taken further,
would lead not to the break-up of the Poor Law but to a more pur-
poseful and efficaceous system of relief. Booth's proposal for a
weekly pension of 7 shillings that was available at the age of seventy
to everyone who had not previously received poor relief was couched
in the language of less-eligibility. By this means the deserving poor
would be removed from the workhouse to live in the community. The
prospect of such payment, he argued, would act not only as an incentive to resist dependency but also serve to strengthen family life. Non-
contributory old age pensions, so far from encouraging dissipation,
would promote thrift and foster the growth of a population that was
steeled in the discipline of deterrence. Equally important, pensions reform would make possible the final abolition of outrelief which,
wrote Booth, 'I regard as essential'. Pensions, in short, would reduce
the burdens on the Poor Law and private charity simplifying the
problems each had to treat and leading to united and more effective
action in dealing with distress and destitution. [10, Final Volume
pp. 142–50].

SOCIAL INQUIRY AND SOCIAL ACTION

Socialism and the New Liberalism were fattened on social research.
Contemporary thinking about poverty and well-being was deeply influenced by the disclosures of Booth and his successors. The Life and
Labour Inquiry grew out of and fed the reaction against a political
economy that seemed wanting in reality and morality. Booth's researches had shown that, far from constituting part of the fixed order
of things, poverty was definable, measurable and capable of remedial
action. His reputation was carried forward by the ex-members of his
team who secured influential positions in the public service and by
subsequent social investigators who sought his guidance and support.
Chief among them was the Quaker philanthropist B. S. Rowntree
who undertook a comparable study of poverty in York in 1899.
Rowntree's inquiry, published three years later as *Poverty, A Study of
Town Life*, attended closely to the causes of poverty and showed that
one-third of the poor had incomes too low for physical fitness and
that nearly three-quarters of these inadequate family incomes came
from full-time regular earnings. Rowntree, like Booth, employed a
relative definition of poverty in which observed living conditions
were compared with approved or conventional understandings of
poverty [159]. Rowntree's approach, though, was innovatory in three

respects. First, in its incorporation of nutritional science to measure poverty in terms of the ability to meet a minimum standard of physiological health and efficiency. Second, in its distinction between primary and secondary poverty (i.e., poverty resulting from insufficiency of income and poverty resulting from inefficient expenditure) to show how the life-style of the poor was in part caused by low income and not by improvidence. Third, in its idea of the poverty cycle which showed that people moved in and out of poverty according to the age and earning-power of themselves and their children. Rowntree's survey, while it showed that large families accounted for a fifth of those who were found to be in primary poverty, also suggested that poverty was not a condition that separated the poor from the working class but a phase through which individuals passed in the course of their lives [16].

Social research as undertaken by Booth and Rowntree questioned the assumptions of 1834. The idea that jobs were available for all at some wage level and that unemployment was therefore an expression of individual laziness was revealed as too simplistic to account for the complexities which the Booth and Rowntree inquiries had revealed. Neither author in reaching their conclusions saw the need to jettison traditional values associated with industry, thrift and character. The scope for personal responsibility in both cases was not diminished by the recognition that certain forms of distress and deprivation were incapable of individual remedy and required the resources of the state as part of the solution. The social question, it was clear, was not reducible to the repression of pauperism. Measures were required to raise living standards to combat preventible misery, reduce class tension and promote the industrial and social efficiency essential to the maintenance of British imperial power.

THE ROYAL COMMISSION ON THE POOR LAWS, 1905-9

Booth was aware that pensions and poor law reform, unless taken in tandem, would, as Alfred Marshall put it, result in 'a most expensive garment made up of patches' [141 *p. 371*]. In joining the newly created Royal Commission on the Poor Laws in 1905, he hoped to contribute towards the formation of a more unified social policy. The case for such initiative was readily conceded. The Poor Law neither satisfied the devotees of deterrence nor appeased the champions of a modern social service state. The process of piecemeal adjustment, it was alleged, had left the New Poor Law without a principle and 'made of it a monstrosity' [25 *p. 528*]. The Poor Law was not only a

failure, it was an expensive failure. The cost of the Poor Law in England and Wales rose from 7s. ¼d. (about 35p) per head of the
pop-ulation in 1871–72 to 8s. 7 ¼d. (about 43p) per head of the population in 1905–6, an increase of more than 25 per cent. In the ten years
ending 1905–6 the mean annual expenditure per pauper rose by more
than 50 per cent from £9. 8s. 11d. (about £9. 45p) to £14 13s. 11d.
(about £14. 70p).

The Royal Commission on the Poor Laws and Relief of Distress
was appointed in 1905 at the fag end of a Conservative Government
that had quite lost its way in social policy. Its remit was to report on
'Everything which apertains to...the problem of the poor, whether
poor by their own fault, or by temporary lack of employment'. Its
members included a broad range of expert and lay opinion. All stand-
points were represented. The votaries of less eligibility were stoutly
defended by C. S. Loch, Octavia Hill, Helen Bosanquet and three
other members of the Charity Organization Society. The Local Government Board had four representatives, the boards of guardians five;
trade unionists had Francis Chandler, Secretary of the Amalgamated
Society of Carpenters (who was also a former chairman of the
Chorlton-on-Medlock Board of Guardians), and the inmate population had George Lansbury (1859–1940), the Poplar socialist and
future leader of the Labour Party, who pressed for care, consideration
and decency towards paupers at whatever cost. Charles Booth, doyen
of poverty studies, and his erstwhile assistant Beatrice Webb, brought
a new kind of specialist knowledge to the commission's deliberations.
Russell Wakefield, Dean of Norwich, was also a member. The chairman of this formidable body was the Conservative ex-Cabinet
Minister, Lord George Hamilton (1845–1927) [164].

Its inquiries lasted three years in which time some 200 Unions were
visited, 400 institutions inspected, 450 witnesses examined and 900
written statements taken. In all, forty-seven folio volumes were filled
in what was to become one of the most detailed and exacting of official investigations. Being together for so long, though, seems to have
encouraged cleavage rather than consensus. In February 1909, the
Commission issued a Minority Report signed by Webb, Lansbury,
Chandler and Wakefield and a Majority Report signed by the chairman and fourteen others.

There was a good deal of common ground between them. Neither
supported the preservation of the status quo or retention of a separate Poor Law that was wanting uniformity in standards of provision
and administration. Majority and Minority Reports likewise recognized the unnecessary duplication of duties by Poor Law and local

authorities and the general failure to address the problems arising from involuntary poverty. On the prevention of poverty and the role of rehabilitation there was similar agreement. On unemployment and the reorganization of the labour market, too, there was much in common. The introduction of labour exchanges, raising of the school-leaving age and decasualization of labour commanded ready assent from both parties. Majority and Minority Reports, united in their opposition to anything other than means-tested benefits, were also as one in their support for the forcible segregation of those inefficient parasitical elements, the so-called residuum, who were deemed to be incapable of improvement.

The Majority Report [*Doc. 16*] sought a radical reorganization in which the guardians would be superseded by public assistance committees made up of elected representatives from the local authorities and co-opted members from the voluntary sector. The latter, charged with the duties of inquiry and assistance, would help to initiate a co-ordinated relief system to which public and private bodies would contribute in a rational and coherent manner. The Majority Report, for all its commitment to co-operation between the state and private sector, tended to exalt personal over public service and the superiority of organized voluntary action over state assistance. Among its signatories there was no doubt as to who would become the junior member in the post-poor law partnership.

The Minority Report [*Doc. 17*], drafted by Sidney and Beatrice Webb, questioned the efficacy and regenerative potential of a new-style partnership with unpopular bodies like the Charity Organization Society, and in its stead presented a far more engaging case for the 'break up of the poor law'. The Poor Law, they argued, was based on principles that were fundamentally flawed. Destitution, it was claimed, was a social disease which required a preventative approach. Its causes lay beyond the reach of the board of guardians who lacked the resources and the imagination to do any more than palliate the problem. The deterrence principles on which the Poor Law was organized, moreover, were designed to discourage the needy from coming forward for assistance or treatment; too often it seemed as though the primary purpose was to keep them off the rates rather than advance their well-being. The multiform causes of poverty also required greater specialization and sensitivity to different categories of social needs. The recipients of assistance included many different kinds of people – infants and unemployed workmen, school children and aged persons, widows, the sick and the feeble-minded. The boards of guardians were not in a position to deal satisfactorily with all these different classes. The elected local authorities, the Minority Report continued, were better equipped to discharge all such duties apart from unemployment which required national action.

The Royal Commission of 1905–9 invites comparison with its predecessor of 1832–34. In sheer weight of expertise it was head and shoulders above its forebear. Unlike the Poor Law Commission of 1832–34, that of 1905–9 included a large number of appointees who were actively involved with poor law administration. Available, too, were the leading lights in the social movement. Charles Booth thus assumed responsibility for the collection and analysis of poor law statistics while equally weighty projects were allocated to C. S. Loch and Beatrice Webb who was also the moving force behind the special inquiries that were undertaken on behalf of the Commission. In contrast with the Assistant Commissioners of 1832–34, the Special Investigators of 1905–9 found themselves less absorbed with maladministration and more concerned with indigence in connection with pauperism. In short, their researches expanded the scope of the Royal Commission so as to embrace the causes of destitution as well as the nature of pauperism. Why, then, should its outcome have been so unsatisfactory?

The gap between Majority and Minority Reports, though subsequently it came to be viewed as unbridgeable, did not seem so at the time. Beatrice Webb herself thought that, among her fellow commissioners, it was the want of a good lawyer who was expert in the art of negotiation that prevented the submission of a unanimous report. Charles Booth, until forced to retire from public life on grounds of ill-health, tried to find a middle way [137]. Booth sought to extend and develop the mixed economy of welfare by enlarging the scope of charitable assistance and private effort and by the improved co-ordination of the voluntary and public sectors. The Poor Law was not to be broken up but humanized. The term 'workhouse' was to be replaced by 'institution'. Outdoor relief would be abolished and indoor relief known as 'institutional treatment'. Pauperism he regarded as a 'social disease'. The deserving poor were thus to become the 'curable' or 'helpable' poor. Children, the sick and the disabled were to remain within the purview of the Poor Law and to receive provision that was adequate but not provocative so that the thrifty self-supporting worker was not discouraged. Deterrence was to be modified rather than abandoned. Claims for less eligibility would henceforth be satisfied by loss of independence and submission to a 'progressive discipline' which would operate with greater or lesser severity depending upon the individual inmate. Work was to be rational rather than punitive, designed to rehabilitate and restore the pauper to independence. Booth's scheme also provided for the replacement of the poor law guardians by poor law boards appointed by the county councils with representatives from the Local Government Board which was also to exert greater financial control over poor law administration.

Booth, though by no means antagonistic towards the COS, was considered suspect by the defenders of deterrence who regarded his support for redistributive taxation on behalf of the aged poor as rank socialism. The government's ill-timed announcement in 1907 of its intention to proceed with pensions legislation came as a surprise to Booth's fellow commissioners who, quite wrongly, considered it proof sufficient of the malign and manipulative enterprise to which he was committed. Booth's intervention, moreover, riled the chairman Lord George Hamilton who felt that he was being upstaged and resented it. Finally, Booth severely underestimated the distance that separated his ideas from those of Beatrice Webb for whom the break-up of the Poor Law had become the key to further progress in social policy and social welfare. 'Booth', as she noted in her diary, 'is more concerned with the question of right treatment than of prevention by better regulated life' [25 *p. 489*]. He also underestimated the gap between Majority and Minority Reports which, in spite of numerous points of agreement, were based on antagonistic social philosophies.

Booth's failure to mediate between the warring camps was to have important consequences. In the first place, it removed the last restriction on Beatrice Webb who, with Sidney's assistance, went all out for an extremely high profile campaign on behalf of the Minority Report. Booth's own proposals, published as *Poor Law Reform* (1910), instead of rallying moderate parties, served merely to deepen divisions. The campaign for the break-up of the Poor Law, conducted by the Webbs and their opponents in the years before the First World War, proved singularly ineffective in forming elite or popular opinion. For the politicians, poor law reform had become too hot to handle; for their constituents employment-related issues seemed more pressing. The Liberal government, with Lloyd George (1863–1945) in the ascendant, decided to bypass the subject and proceed with an insurance-based welfare strategy that was calculated to remove the most pressing sources of need from poor law administration. The decision to do so owed something to the hamstrung Royal Commission and the denial to ministers of a unanimous report to face-down the wealthy and influential local authorities who opposed the rate equalization reforms that were preparatory to meaningful changes in poor law services [136].

CONCLUSION

Indigence was defined by the Poor Law Commission of 1834 as 'the state of a person unable to labour or unable to obtain in return for his labour the means of subsistence'. Poverty, by contrast, was described as 'the state of one, who in order to obtain a mere subsistence, is forced to have recourse to labour'. The assumption of the Poor Law Commission was that the labourer who was physically capable would find work and would earn a wage sufficient to maintain himself and his family. Only the partially or totally disabled who could not demand a full wage were eligible for social support. Poverty was understood to constitute the natural condition of the working class and did not require social intervention. The economic level of the poor was determined by the employment market which lay beyond the boundaries of social reform or government action.

The principles of 1834 assumed a competitive system in which the price of labour was fixed by demand and supply. It was assumed, too, that workers had perfect information on which to make rational decisions about pay and conditions. In this conception, labour was regarded as a set of components that were endlessly rearrangeable. Unemployment, low wages and underemployment were simply part of the system for treating labour components according to their estimated worth in the productive process and of persuading workers to abandon occupations where their services were surplus to requirements. The competitive system, in short, relied upon the bracing influence of wage reductions, supported by threats of unemployment, old age or death, to impel workers to seek new and better markets for their labour and to inculcate in them habits of foresight and thrift. The possibility of a discrepancy between the requirement of a flexible labour supply and the security of the worker was not admitted until the 1880s. The Booth and Rowntree inquiries showed that, for a substantial proportion of the working class, the wage provided neither full maintenance nor the means of meeting the contingencies of life. Of equal importance were their findings respecting the complexity of social problems. Pauperism had been unpacked. For a minority it was a voluntary condition; for most the chief sources of distress lay in unemployment and underemployment and in sickness, age and misfortune. Self-maintenance required measures beyond the repression of pauperism to raise incomes and promote national efficiency.

This implied a redefined role for the Poor Law in the mixed economy of welfare. The failure of the Royal Commission of 1905–9 to agree on that role left the nation without an acceptable system of social service and without a broader vision of what such a service could be.

PART THREE: ASSESSMENT

6 PROBLEMS AND PROSPECTS

HISTORIANS AND THE POOR LAW

Poor law ideals formed part of the mentality of the middle classes. The principles of 1834 with their distinctive social imagery and assumptions about the nature and purpose of public action rapidly became part of the intellectual baggage of Victorian Britain. The New Poor Law in this perspective was more than a matter of administrative reform. W. N. Molesworth (1816–1890), author of the best-selling *History of England from 1830–1874*, wrote of it as an act of deliverance from insolvency and insurrection and a defining moment in the formation of the age of progress. Poor law reform, in his account, was identified with the movement from darkness and disorder towards virtue and enlightenment. The Old Poor Law was associated with national ruin; the New Poor Law with national improvement. Under the Old Poor Law the poor were out of control; under the New they were properly regulated. Chadwick thus deserved well of his countrymen. Extravagance had been checked and order restored. Fears of a descent into the chaos and confusion of the unreformed era, which revived whenever the economy faltered or unforeseen emergency put pressure on local expenditure, underscored the seminal and uplifting character of the legislation of 1834.

Modern historians take a different view. Today the principles of 1834 have few defenders. There is no reputable historian who regards them as praiseworthy or progressive. The consensus is that the Poor Laws were an egregious error, a ghastly mistake, and a dark phase in the development of social policy. R. H. Tawney (1880–1962) criticized the Report of the Royal Commission of 1834 as 'wildly unhistorical' [156 *p. 269*], to which Mark Blaug added the claim that it was also 'wildly unstatistical' [36 *p. 152*]. E. P. Thompson (1924–1993?) called it 'the most sustained attempt to impose an ideological dogma, in defiance of the evidence of human need, in English history' [157 *p. 267*]. The commissioners, it is often said, were crude ideologues, who had made up their mind in advance of the evidence. No attempt to analyse the causes and nature of poverty was undertaken. Problems arising from structural economic change were passed through the distorting lens of political economy. Destitution thus became a form of individual moral delinquency and poverty a product of maladministration. Deterrence was the solution. Abolish outrelief, abandon wage subsidies, force the able-bodied off the rates and into the labour market and destitution would disappear. These far-reaching recommendations were not the fruit of patient inquiry and careful deliberation. Quite the contrary. Research, though extensive, provided an information-base that was too large to digest and impossible to evaluate in the time available. The commissioners, in compiling their report, drew selectively upon the information that had been gathered to illustrate their arguments. The enormous quantity of statistical evidence which had been acquired was ignored. Modern scholars are generally agreed that the research conducted by the Royal Commission on the Poor Laws served to confirm preconceived positions rather than to guide, illuminate and inform social policy.

In many respects all such writings are an enlargement and amplification of criticisms advanced many years earlier. The central text here is Sidney and Beatrice Webb's monumental history of poor relief. *English Poor Law Policy*, published in 1910, includes a chronological analysis of the development of public policy and is also a preview of their *English Poor Law History*, a three-volume study published between 1927 and 1929. The first of these was devoted to the Old Poor Law; the second and third volumes traced developments from the inception of the New Poor Law down to the abolition of the boards of guardians nearly one hundred years later [24, 25, 33]. The Webbs, unlike professional historians who pass their careers in the academe, occupied several overlapping roles as theorists of Fabian Socialism, social investigators and social reformers. The Webbs, too, were great entertainers. Their West End salon, in which gastronomy came a poor second to political economy, was noted as much for its austerity as for its conversation. Sidney also served as a minister in the first Labour Government; while Beatrice, as writer and broadcaster, never wanted for an audience. Their historical inquiries were not uninfluenced by these wider interests.

The Webbs' belief in the inevitability of collectivism and the primacy of institutions as agents of historical change, accounts for their administrative approach to the study of poor relief while their active participation as poor law reformers gave their writings a distinctive political purpose. The Webbs set out to show how the principles of

1834 had been abandoned and the relief of destitution replaced by a policy of preventative and curative treatment. The Poor Law Report of 1834, they claimed, identified three basic principles: first, that the treatment of paupers should be nationally uniform; second, that their conditions should be made 'less eligible' than that of the lowest paid worker in independent employment; and, third, that outdoor relief should be reduced and replaced by relief inside the workhouse. The Webbs then traced the development of policy under the central authority to point out the discrepancies and contradictions that arose in the application of the principles of 1834 and to show how they had been supplanted by the emergence of a new set of principles. Curative treatment, the first of these, was the antithesis of the principle of less eligibility. The second, the principle of universal provision, referred to the creation of services designed to achieve certain minimum living standards. The third principle, that of compulsion, required that the individual did not neglect the opportunities for a better life for themselves and their families arising from state provision. These sets of principles, it was argued, constituted two opposed philosophies. That of the nineteenth century was individualist and market-orientated and denied any obligation on the part of the community; that of the twentieth implied a new form of mutuality between the state and the individual and a new social ethic.This schematic account, presented in 1907 as the first of Beatrice Webb's historical memoranda for the Royal Commission on the Poor Laws, supplied the organizing framework of the Webbs' subsequent historical writings.

Contemporaries were critical. Helen Bosanquet charged them with having constructed a poor law history that was little more than a vehicle for the realization of their own programmes and ambitions. The progressive movement from repression to prevention by which the Webbs set such great store was a fiction. The Webbs, she claimed, had been too narrow in the range of their sources, too centralist in their perspective and too selective with the use of evidence to sustain their analysis. She could detect no sudden breaks or changes in policy and no evidence for any repudiation of the principles of national uniformity or less eligibility. Curative treatment, so far from a new principle, was a natural outgrowth of the principles of 1834 and the practices that had developed from them, while the so-called principle of universal provision was no more than a confusing construction which had been mischievously inserted into poor law history [136].

Modern historians, too, counsel caution in the use of their writings. If less caustic than Mrs Bosanquet, they are often no less critical. Some include inferior scholarship in their indictment; others focus upon misrepresentation and want of perspective. Neither claim lacks substance. Research for *English Poor Law History* was too heavily reliant upon the historical inquiries initiated by Beatrice twenty years earlier for the Royal Commission on the Poor Laws of 1905–9. At the time of writing, the Webbs were an old couple in a hurry, leading busy public lives which left little time for research or reflection. Still hoping to influence social policy, they sought to complete their poor law history as a contribution to the reform round that was set in motion by Neville Chamberlain in the late 1920s. This forced them into a punishing timetable with limited scope for the revision of dated research or the inclusion of the fresh information they had gathered. *English Poor Law History* was, in consequence, a high-pressured production that was more influenced by contemporary debates about unemployment and social reform than by the requirements of historical scholarship [130].

The Webbs as historians of poor relief have also been criticized for the construction of an idealized account that cannot explain the formation of new policies or the creation of the instruments, procedures and personnel that were required to give them effect [163]. Modern scholars agree that there was no uniform transition to a curative poor law regime and that the authorities pursued several distinct relief strategies at the same time. Nor do they suppose that policy makers kept to hand a copy of 'the principles of 1834' even though initiatives were invariably justified by reference to an imagined account of them. Poor law history, then, cannot be written as a simple progression from deterrence to treatment. Repression was never abolished. Unemployed men were thus excluded from those eligible for relief by 1850. Similarly, a repressive strategy for disciplining paupers in the new workhouses was pursued relentlessly down to 1870; thereafter repression was extended to new classes of pauper while a new strategy of classification and treatment was directed at indoor paupers. The separation of indoor from outdoor relief strategies and the subdivision of material into items like pauper education, medical relief and vagrancy, as presented by the Webbs, obscures the overall shape and structure of poor law policies, the relationships between them and the ways in which they fitted together.

The Webbs as historians, wrote Mrs Bosanquet, were guilty of misrepresentation. In a review of *English Poor Law Policy*, published in the *Economic Journal* in 1910, she castigated the authors for a narrow administrative approach and failure to attend to the adaptation of the New Poor Law to local conditions. This has since become a standing criticism of the Webbs and their work. The need for greater sensitivity to regional and local diversity has, in the past forty years or so, given rise to a spectacular growth in studies which seek to place poor law history in its economic, social and political context. Our understanding has, in consequence, gained in both breadth and depth. Studies of the implementation of the Poor Law Amendment Act in north east Lancashire, Cumbria, Tyneside and East Anglia, for example, suggest a greater continuity in relief practice between the Old and New Poor Laws than was once imagined and imply a diminished importance for the reformed poor law in the development of social policy [56, 58, 64, 70].

Particularly interesting has been the exploration of elite responses to the New Poor Law in the localities. Whether it was welcomed depended partly on financial considerations – poor rates pressed with greater severity on southern as compared with northern rent rolls – upon the strength of local paternalism and antipathy to outside intervention, but above all on the demand for social discipline. This seems to have been greatest in those areas which had recently been exposed to riot, unrest and disturbance. Consequently, some authorities have identified social control as the dominant influence upon the creation and implementation of the New Poor Law. The provisions of the Act of 1834 which allowed JPs in the counties to act as *ex-officio* guardians, it is claimed, enlarged the influence of the landed gentry both in their own person and through their agents or tenants on boards of guardians [57, 100]. This case, argued so forcefully by Anthony Brundage, is not without critics who point out that the argument rests upon evidence drawn from Northamptonshire and the east Midlands and does not possess a wider applicability beyond those counties. Experience elsewhere, it is noted, showed that once the new poor law unions had been successfully launched, gentry and aristocratic participation diminished [109]. Farmers and tradesmen assumed the leadership of boards of guardians which often became the cockpit of local party politics [116]. The relief system, then, had dynamism as well as diversity.

Local studies also remind us that uniformity in poor law administration was an aspiration rather than an achievement. The idea of a nineteenth-century revolution in government* is called into question by the failure to regularize local poor relief practices in line with Benthamite precept [135, 147]. There seems to have been considerable variation from region to region and within and between unions. Some dissimilarities can be explained by differing traditions of poor relief before 1834, by urban-rural differences and by the variation in capacity constraints that came from the influence of social structure upon rateable values (and hence upon union revenues). Durham and Northumberland, with its mixed industrial economy, was thus more receptive to the New Poor Law than the narrowly-based textile towns of Lancashire and the West Riding. By 1841 every Durham union had a new or refurbished workhouse. Lancashire and Yorkshire, by contrast, were still completing their building programmes in the 1860s. Priorities in relief practice were also affected by external changes in the environment. The shift from the lavish to the parsimonious in the north-east between the 1830s and 1840s, for example, was an adjustment brought about by economic recession, acute unemployment and rising rates [59]. Recurrent agrarian depression and its impact upon the surplus labour problem exerted an equally important influence upon social administration in East Anglia [43].

Economic considerations are also important in understanding regional contrasts in poor relief. Patterns of real expenditure, for example, diverged markedly around mid-century especially between London and the industrial regions. The singularity of the metropolis was also evident in the greater importance attached to indoor relief in London compared with relief practice in Lancashire or the West Riding [61]. In the 1850s and 1860s out-relief as a proportion of total expenditure was lower in London than in other regions while indoor relief was always higher. The greater reluctance of northern guardians to implement the workhouse test was not simply a form of resistance to administrative centralism but also an expression of employer attitudes towards poor law administration. Where, as in the North, large employers continued to dominate poor law policy, outdoor relief was used to subsidize the labour force during periods of high unemployment.

Enough has now been written to indicate the value of local studies. Something, though, remains to be said about the downside of such writing. The substantial literature thus created has by its sheer bulk and variety become an obstacle to the advancement of knowledge. As one historian has recently observed 'there is no single history of the New Poor Law but instead several different histories of distinctive institutional and regional practices' [61 *p. 210*]. Two features give further cause for concern. Particularly puzzling are the discrepant estimates of the importance of outdoor relief. Local studies have in general tended to support the consensus that the New Poor Law failed to abolish outdoor relief [19, 20, 21, 153]. A dissident view maintains the contrary. A wealth of statistical information is presented by Karel Williams in support of the contention that outdoor relief for able-bodied adult men was abolished by 1850 [163]. These claims have not been disproved. No engagement has taken place [cf. 20, 26]. The profession has in general praised the statistical resource which has been created but ignored the conclusions derived from it.

The key issue concerns the character of poor law statistics and above all the system of classification and the manner of compilation. Williams, it must be said, has not researched poor law statistics at the point of production or transmission. His case for the abolition of out-door relief is built upon the figures published by the central authority. Is it possible that the able-bodied male unemployed were relieved but misrepresented and returned under the various sickness exception clauses of the relief prohibitory orders of 1844 and 1852? Under these clauses, outdoor relief could be made available to the sick, in cases of 'sudden and urgent necessity' and in cases of 'sickness, accident and mental incapacity'. Guardians were also empowered to dispense outdoor relief provided such cases were reported to the central authority for approval. Guardians who were so minded might easily exploit these discretionary powers to frustrate the bureaucrats in London. As Richard Thompson notes of poor law administration in Cumbria 'there was ample scope for "stretching" the categories of exemption' [70 *p. 128*]. Williams argues that such practices could not have been extensive and directs his attack at those local studies in which the argument for the defeat of national policy rests upon the wilful evasion of boards of guardians. For this to be plausible it would have been necessary to conceal unemployment-related relief under another category. Having searched all the available categories, Williams can find no evidence of concealment. The published figures, which indicate the virtual abolition of outdoor relief by 1850, must he concludes, be correct. Sixteen years have passed since Williams's account was published. In that time interesting work on the statistics of pauperism as a surrogate measure of unemployment has been completed [47, 55]. No fresh research on how the figures were originated and processed has been undertaken, however.

Equally unsatisfactory is the tendency to minimize differences between the unreformed and reformed relief systems [18]. Some scholars have, indeed, lodged a protest against 'a new orthodoxy that threatens to explain away the New Poor Law altogether' [52 *p. 38*]. Close study of the implementation of the Poor Law Amendment Act in Bedfordshire serves to illustrate the massive changes wrought by the new legislation in the lives of the poor. Under the Old Poor Law the parish was the focal point of a system that was organized and managed by local people within small communities in which social relations were regulated by customary notions of duty and obligation. No such sense of mutuality animated the reformed Poor Law. The organization and assumptions of the New Poor Law were, if anything, the very antithesis of local accountability. The parish was engulfed within vast new unions that were staffed by 'stranger' professionals brought in from outside the community under the aegis of equally distant boards of guardians. The old arrangements gave ready access to those in authority; the new arrangements were altogether more exclusive. The introduction of impersonal bureaucratic procedures to replace the direct relations between governors and governed was experienced by the poor as a significant deprivation. Such changes, it has been suggested, must be viewed as part of a larger process in which the New Poor Law appears as a milestone on the road towards a modern market-orientated rural elite [140]. If this is so, it would also explain why, as Brundridge maintains, poor law reform was welcomed as a means of strengthening the power of traditional landowners over the localities [102]. However, research is at present insufficient to judge the merits of these various viewpoints. The geography of gentry modernization remains to be established as do the changes in social relations that are patterned upon it.

THE PLACE OF THE POOR LAW IN MODERN BRITISH HISTORY

What are we to make of the Victorian Poor Law? How does it relate to current understandings of social policy? Questions concerning the place of the Poor Law in the development of social administration and social welfare have been of signal importance in modern poor law studies. Historians in seeking to establish a coherent connection between past and present sometimes tend to align the Victorian poor law with the emergence of the welfare state and present the one as the natural outgrowth of the other [117]. The welfare state, in this interpretation, was created as a reaction to the harshness and cruelty of the New Poor Law [123]. The key assumption here, that the Poor Law was inhumanity writ large, has not passed without challenge [152]. It is argued by some historians that much contemporary criticism was exaggerated and self-serving in character and that conditions were so varied as to render all such judgements unsound. Cruelty, moreover, is a relative concept. Others, without seeking to deny the cruelty of the Poor Law, prefer to focus upon its positive contribution to the modern welfare state. In this perspective the workhouse figures as a 'welfare institution', the cradle of the National Health Service, source of enlightened education and the harbinger of modern institutional care [117, 89, 90, 17]. The Poor Law, they argue, became progressive in spite of itself.

How and why this change came about remains the subject of continuing research. However, some historians argue that the idea of a radical transition is itself illusory and dispute the alleged humanizing of the Poor Law in the late-nineteenth century. The 'crusade against outdoor relief', we are reminded, sharply curtailed the number of people receiving relief and is proof positive against any softening of the commitment to deterrence. So, far from an enlargement in the scope of social provision, the period after 1870 saw a tightening in the administration of poor relief. Political criticism and active opposition were forestalled by the tax changes initiated by the Union Chargeability Act of 1865 which permitted the improvement in workhouse facilities so as to secure the restriction of outrelief and public acceptance of indoor relief [47]. The argument, however, rests upon econometric modelling and, though plausible, is not proven.

One way forward is to focus upon the bureaucratic origins of the welfare state. Here the New Poor Law appears as an exemplification of the process of administrative reform whereby the state equipped itself with the means to deal with the social and economic problems arising from the unplanned growth of an industrial urban society. The theme is developed at length in David Roberts's *The Victorian Origins of the Welfare State* (1960), in which poor law reform is presented as a central feature of that enlarged capacity for social intervention that was to make Britain one of the most innovative and creative of welfare states [151]. The discrepancy between precept and practice in poor law administration – above all, the want of uniformity and sheer diversity of local practices – has prompted some scholars to question the validity of this interpretation. The Poor Law, it is argued, so far from a perfect model of administrative centralism, was its very negation. 'If anything', concludes Derek Fraser, 'twentieth century welfare based on common standards derived from a bureaucratic reaction against the diversity of the Poor Law' [117 *p.* 23]. More telling is the conceptual confusion that lies beneath such arguments. Scholars nowadays argue for a distinction between a 'social service state' characterized by minimal national standards of provision for the poor and a 'welfare state' defined by an explicit commitment to a comprehensive scheme of income maintenance and an optimal level of service for the whole population. On this basis the welfare state is very largely a post-Second World War phenomenon.

How the New Poor Law can be understood in terms of 'the Victorian origins of the welfare state' remains unclear.

The scope and character of public action raises further issues about the place of the Poor Law in British history. The Poor Law is important because it provided the institutional framework and principles for most publicly financed welfare provision in Victorian Britain. Until the passage of the Poor Law Amendment Act of 1834, the basis of social policy had rested on the Elizabethan legislation of 1601, which made it obligatory on the parish to provide relief and work. The New Poor Law abandoned this form of repressive paternalism in favour of a liberal conception in which the individual was free to pursue his or her fortune and in which success or failure was a matter of personal responsibility. The Act of 1834 brought rigour and system to the management of the poor. The allegedly wasteful and irrational practices of the Old Poor Law, above all, the misconceived promise of a living wage held out by the justices at Speenhamland, were swept away. In its place came the workhouse system and the war on outdoor relief. From that point onwards, the question of wages was entirely separate from that of charity: and the rate left to fluctuate in accordance with the law of demand and supply. The New Poor Law, in abandoning the Elizabethan legislation, reduced rather than enlarged the notion of the state's responsibility for the disadvantaged and the poor. Its narrowness was striking. Questions concerning the possible connection of social reform with broader social issues such as the improvement of labour force efficiency or industrial adjustment to social needs and working conditions, were submerged beneath a petty preoccupation with the implications of poverty for local taxation. Attendant problems were dealt with in a piecemeal fashion: social reform proceeded as though each item were a special case, each with its own justification. No coherent image of Britain, either as a social service or as a welfare state, emerged. The Poor Law Amendment Act, directed at the stratospheric rise in poor relief between 1770 and 1802, was first and foremost an economy measure. The wider implications of the Speenhamland decision for social policy were scarcely considered.

In truth, it makes more sense to think of the legislation of 1834 as the expression of a defensive strategy to relieve the landed interest of the cost of caring for the victims of economic and industrial change. To this end, an aristocratic regime sanctioned the creation of a freestanding organization to work under the control of the legislature but independently of the machinery of local government. Such, in outline, is the argument of Douglas E. Ashford. In *The Emergence of the Wel-*

fare States (1986) he supplies a comparative analysis of developments in Europe and North America to show how the New Poor Law served to close down opportunities for creative public action, and how in terms of state capacity it represented a dead-end or cul-de-sac from which the British had to escape before progress could be resumed [98].

Even if we find his conclusions too sweeping, it must be said that an approach which emphasizes the ways in which differing state capacities are created is more helpful than approaches which try to present the relationship between the poor law and the welfare state in terms of a transition from one form of social control to another that was different in shape but similar in function. The problem here is that social control means different things to different scholars [107, 128, 158]. Apart from a want of clarity and consensus in defining the concept, there is considerable uncertainty in identifying the means through which control was exercised – personal, ideological, institutional – and no idea of how the various players came to learn their prescribed parts. As an explanatory device it seems to create more problems than it solves.

THE POOR AND THE POOR LAW

A standing criticism of the current approach to poor law history is that it is concerned with policy rather than people, with what legislators and officials thought should happen rather than with the experiences of ordinary people. Paupers are too often presented as helpless, hapless and hopeless sorts who, on entering the workhouse, relinquished their independence to become the victims rather than the makers of history. Mainstream labour history with its emphasis upon the working class as social agents has found little of interest inside the workhouse. Historians of social policy, with rather different priorities, have become interested in the nature of the workhouse regime and the relationships it sustained. M. A. Crowther, drawing upon the work of American sociologist Ervin Goffman (1922–1982), likens the workhouse to a 'total institution' in which groups of people are isolated from wider society and bureaucratically processed with inmates required to eat, sleep, work and play within the confines of the same institution. Goffman, though primarily concerned with mental hospitals, thought that the idea was generalizable to encompass prisons, concentration camps, boarding schools, barracks and monasteries. His analysis of relationships within such institutions served to reveal the tendency towards the bureaucratic regimentation and manipulation of the inmates in the interests of the staff. Goffman's ideas, constitute an analytical framework in which the institutional history of the Poor Law can usefully be situated [17]. Valuable, too, are the insights to be gained from French social theorist Michel Foucault (1926–1984) who studied the birth of the prison to show how the new reformatory regime – characterized by observation, classification, surveillance, hierarchy, rules, discipline and regulation – became the model for the whole of modern society [105]. Crowther thus invites us to consider the workhouse as part of a larger pattern of incarceration from which modern residential management is a direct descendant. The emphasis of her work, as of other historians who have been similarly influenced, is upon those aspects of the workhouse system that are primarily concerned with the management of the poor rather than upon the poor themselves [108]. This emphasis is all the more surprising in view of Goffman's insistence upon the failure of total institutions and the relative autonomy created by the inmates to avoid regulation and surveillance. The extent to which the inmate's personality was moulded by the workhouse regime in fact resists simple summary. Dependency, passivity and lethargy, the usual effects of institutionalization, must, if they applied at all, have applied only to a minority of the inmate population; for the evidence we have on turnover within the workhouse suggests that almost 80 per cent of admissions were emergency cases of people who left within weeks. Moreover, the growth of specialization and progressive withdrawal of different groups from the workhouse – children, the elderly, the sick, etc. – meant that the scope for reformation increasingly diminished as the century wore on. Even in respect of those who were more or less permanently domiciled in the workhouse, little is known of the social and cultural resources of the residents in relation to possible changes in personal identity. Nor has there been any exploration of the significance of performance and non-performance of prescribed roles. It may be, as is often claimed, that the necessary documentation does not exist or cannot be located. No further progress is possible if this is the case; if it is not, future generations will condemn us as hopelessly defeatist or just plain daft.

The call for a history of dependency, made by Peter Hennock some twenty years ago, still awaits a proper response. Poor law policy makers, who sought to influence the conduct of the poor, seem to have shown rather more interest in the reactions of recipients than have modern historians. It is easy to believe that the records of the New Poor Law consist of nothing but statutes, orders, circulars, minutes, general reports and official letters. This is not so. The central authority for England and Wales, though unable to intervene in particular cases, preserved a large number of individual complaints in its files and sometimes referred them to the relevant poor law union for comment and clarification. Local records, too, are often more tractable than is generally imagined. The dominant institutional approach to poor law history, then, need not preclude an attempt to engage with the experience of applicants and recipients of relief and with the way it cross-cuts the life history of the working classes [97]. Closer attention to popular feelings and attitudes might also aid our understanding of the relationship between poor relief and modern welfare practices. The Edwardian Poor Law, so often presented as the welfare state in embryo, was unacceptable to citizen workers who felt that it was hopelessly compromised by its previous associations. If this is the case, the welfare state must be seen as an alternative to the Poor Law rather than an extension of it; with its chief claim to popular support arising from the fact that it was free from the taint of pauperism and in no way identified with poor law administration.

PART FOUR: DOCUMENTS

DOCUMENT 1   POPULATION AND POVERTY, 1798

Thomas Robert Malthus (1766–1834) served as a clergyman and professor of political economy. The following is from one of the seminal texts of Victorian social theory.

I feel no doubt whatever that the parish laws of England have contributed to raise the price of provisions and to lower the real price of labour. They have therefore contributed to impoverish that class of people whose only possession is their labour. It is also difficult to suppose that they have not powerfully contributed to generate that carelessness and want of frugality observable among the poor, so contrary to the disposition frequently to be remarked among petty tradesmen and small farmers. The labouring poor to use a vulgar expression seem always to live from hand to mouth. Their present wants employ their whole attention, and they seldom think of the future. Even when they have an opportunity of saving they seldom exercise it, but all that is beyond their present necessities goes . . . to the ale-house. The poor-laws of England may therefore be said to diminish both the power and the will to save among the common people, and thus to weaken one of the strongest incentives to sobriety and industry, and consequently to happiness . . . .

The poor-laws of England were undoubtedly instituted for the most benevolent purpose, but there is great reason to think that they have not succeeded in their intention. They certainly mitigate some cases of very severe distress which might otherwise occur, yet the state of the poor who are supported by parishes, considered in all its circumstances, is very far from being free from misery. But one of the principal objections to them is that for this assistance which some of the poor receive, in itself almost a doubtful blessing, the common people of England is subjected to a set of grating, inconvenient and tyrannical laws, totally inconsistent with the genuine spirit of the constitution. The whole business of settlements, even in its present amended form, is utterly contradictory to all ideas of freedom. The parish persecution of men whose families are likely to become chargeable, and of poor women who are near lying-in, is a most disgraceful and disgusting tyranny. And the obstructions continually occasioned in the market of labour by these laws, have a constant tendency to add to the difficulties of those who are struggling to support themselves without assistance . . . .

The evils attendant on the poor-laws are in some degree irremediable. If assistance be distributed to a certain class of people, a power must be given somewhere of discriminating the proper objects and of managing the concerns of the institutions that are necessary, but any great interference with the affairs of other people, is a species of tyranny, and in the common course of things the exercise of this power may be expected to become grating to those who are driven to ask for support. The tyranny of Justices, Churchwardens and Overseers, is a common complaint among the poor, but the fault does not lie so much in these persons, who probably before they were in power, were not worse than other people, but in the nature of all such institutions.

The evil is perhaps gone too far to be remedied, but I . . . doubt . . . that if the poor-laws had never existed, though there might have been a few more instances of very severe distress, yet that the aggregate mass of happiness among the common people would have been much greater than it is at present.

Source: T. R. Malthus, [13], pp. 86–7, 91–4.

DOCUMENT 2   REPORT OF THE ROYAL COMMISSION ON THE POOR LAWS, 1834

The rationale of the New Poor Law is summarized in the following text.

Remedial measures

The most pressing of the evils which we have described are those connected with the relief of the able-bodied. They are the evils, therefore, for which we shall first propose remedies.

If we believed the evils stated in the previous part of the Report, or evils resembling or even approaching them, to be necessarily incidental to the compulsory relief of the able-bodied, we should not hesitate in recommending its entire abolition. But we do not believe these evils to be its necessary consequences. We believe that under strict regulations, adequately enforced, such relief may be afforded safely and even beneficially.

In all extensive communities, circumstances will occur in which an individual, by the failure of his means of subsistence, will be exposed to the danger of perishing. To refuse relief, and at the same time to punish mendicity when it cannot be proved that the offender could have obtained subsistence by labour, is repugnant to the common sentiments of mankind; it is repugnant to them to punish even depredation, apparently committed as the only resource against want.

In all extensive civilized communities, therefore, the occurrence of extreme necessity is prevented by alms-giving, by public institutions supported by endowments or voluntary contributions, or by a provision partly voluntary and partly compulsory, or by a provision entirely compulsory, which may exclude the pretext of mendicancy.

But in no part of Europe except England has it been thought fit that the provision, whether compulsory or voluntary, should be applied to more than the relief of *indigence*, the state of a person unable to labour, or unable to obtain, in return for his labour, the means of subsistence. It has never been deemed expedient that the provision should extend to the relief of *poverty*; that is, the state of one who, in order to obtain a mere subsistence, is forced to have recourse to labour.

From the evidence collected under this Commission, we are induced to believe that a compulsory provision for the relief of the indigent can be generally administered on a sound and well-defined principle; and that under the operation of this principle, the assurance that no one need perish from want may be rendered more complete than at present, and the mendicant and vagrant repressed by disarming them of their weapon – the plea of impending starvation.

It may be assumed that in the administration of relief the public is warranted in imposing such conditions on the individual relief as are conducive to the benefit either of the individual himself, or of the country at large, at whose expense he is to be relieved.

The first and most essential of all conditions, a principle which we find universally admitted, even by those whose practice is at variance with it, is that his situation on the whole shall not be made really or apparently so eligible as the situation of the independent labourer of the lowest class. Throughout the evidence it is shown that in proportion as the condition of any pauper class is elevated above the condition of independent labourers, the condition of the independent class is depressed; their industry is impaired, their employment becomes unsteady, and its remuneration in wages is diminished. Such persons, therefore, are under the strongest inducements to quit the less eligible class of labourers and enter the more eligible class of paupers. The converse is the effect when the pauper class is placed in its proper position, below the condition of the independent labourer. Every penny bestowed that tends to render the condition of the pauper more eligible than that of the independent labourer, is a bounty on indolence and vice. We have found that as the poor's rates are at present administered, they operate as bounties of this description, to the amount of several millions annually . . . .

Principle of administering relief to the indigent

From the above evidence it appears that wherever the principle which we have thus stated has been carried into effect, either wholly or partially, its introduction has been beneficial to the class for whose benefit poor laws exist. We have seen that in every instance in which the able-bodied labourers have been rendered independent of partial relief or of relief otherwise than in a well-regulated work house:

1. Their industry has been restored and improved.
2. Frugal habits have been created or strengthened.
3. The permanent demand for their labour has increased.
4. And the increase has been such, that their wages, so far from being depressed by the increased amount of labour in the market, have in general advanced.
5. The number of improvident and wretched marriages has diminished.
6. Their discontent has been abated, and their moral and social condition in every way improved.

Principle of legislation

Results so important would, even with a view to the interest of that class exclusively, afford sufficient ground for the general introduction of the principle of administration under which those results have been produced. Considering the extensive benefits to be anticipated from the adoption of measures founded on principles already tried and found beneficial, and warned at every part of the inquiry by the failure of previous legislation, we shall, in the suggestion of specific remedies, endeavour not to depart from the firm ground of actual experience.

We therefore submit, as the general principle of legislation on this subject, in the present condition of the country:

That those modes of administering relief which have been tried wholly or partially, and have produced beneficial effects in some Districts, be introduced, with modifications according to local circumstances, and carried into complete execution in all.

The chief specific measures which we recommend for effecting these purposes, are-

FIRST, THAT EXCEPT AS TO MEDICAL ATTENDANCE, AND SUBJECT TO THE EXCEPTION RESPECTING APPRENTICESHIP HEREIN AFTER STATED, ALL RELIEF WHATEVER TO ABLEBODIED PERSONS OR TO THEIR FAMILIES, OTHERWISE THAN IN WELL-REGULATED WORKHOUSES (i.e., PLACES WHERE THEY MAY BE SET TO WORK ACCORDING TO THE SPIRIT AND INTENTION OF THE 43 ELIZABETH) SHALL BE DECLARED UNLAWFUL, AND SHALL CEASE, IN MANNER AND AT PERIODS HEREAFTER SPECIFIED; AND THAT ALL RELIEF AFFORDED IN RESPECT OF CHILDREN UNDER THE AGE OF SIXTEEN SHALL BE CONSIDERED AS AFFORDED TO THEIR PARENTS.

Source: Report of the Royal Commission on the Poor Laws, 1834, XXVII, (1834), pp. 127, 146–7.

DOCUMENT 3 OUTDOOR RELIEF PROHIBITORY ORDER, DECEMBER 1844

The following registers the direction of policy under the New Poor Law. Its effect, though, cannot be inferred from the mere statement of aims and objects.

ARTICLE 1. Every able-bodied person, male or female, requiring relief from any Parish within any of the said Unions, shall be relieved wholly in the Workhouse of the Union, together with such of the family of every such able-bodied person as may be resident with him or her, and may not be in employment, and together with the wife of every such able-bodied male person, if he be a married man, and if she be resident with him; save and except in the following cases:

1st. Where such person shall require relief on account of sudden and urgent necessity.

2d. Where such person shall require relief on account of any sickness, accident, or bodily or mental infirmity affecting such person, or any of his or her family.

3d. Where such person shall require relief for the purpose of defraying the expenses, either wholly or in part, of the burial of any of his or her family.

4th. Where such person, being a widow, shall be in the first six months of her widowhood.

5th. Where such person shall be a widow, and have a legitimate child or legitimate children dependent upon her, and incapable of earning his, her, or their livelihood, and have no illegitimate child born after the commencement of her widowhood.

6th. Where such person shall be confined in any gaol or place of safe custody.

7th. Where such person shall be the wife, or child, of any able-bodied man who shall be in the service of Her Majesty as a soldier, sailor, or marine.

8th. Where any able-bodied person, not being a soldier, sailor, or marine, shall not reside within the Union, but the wife, child, or children of such person shall reside within the same, the Board of Guardians of the Union, according to their discretion, may, subject to the regulation contained in Article 4, afford relief in the Workhouse to such wife, child, or children, or may allow out-door relief for any such child or children being within the age of nurture, and resident with the mother within the Union. . . .

ART. 5. It shall not be lawful for the Guardians, or any of their Officers, or for the Overseer or Overseers of any Parish in the Union, to pay, wholly or in part, the rent of the house or lodging of any pauper, or to apply any portion of the relief ordered to be given to any pauper in payment of any such rent, or to retain any portion of such relief for the purpose of directly or indirectly discharging such rent, in full or in part, for any such pauper.

ART. 6. Provided always, that in case the Guardians of any of the said Unions depart in any particular instance from any of the regulations herein before contained, and within fifteen days after such departure report the same, and the grounds thereof, to the Poor Law Commissioners, and the Poor Law Commissioners approve of such departure, then the relief granted in such particular instance shall, if otherwise lawful, not be deemed to be unlawful, or be subject to be disallowed.

Source: W. C. Glen, [8], pp. 309–12, 317–18.

DOCUMENT 4   PETITION OF JEREMIAH DUNN, 1847

The assumption that the poor had no voice is challenged by the text of the petition printed below. Spellings and punctuation have not been modernized.

To the Honorable the Poor Law Commissioners

The Humble petition of Jeremiah Dunn of No 10

Little Pearl Street, Christchurch, Spitalfields

Sheweth

That your petitioner is a married Man with a Wife and six small children. Is an Irishman by birth but has resided in Spitalfields the last 2 years and in England 24 years and in 1835 & 1836 paid £14 per Annum rent prior to the last 2 years: -
That he is by trade a Weaver but through the depression of the silk line he is reduced to the greatest distress and has been compelled to apply to the White-chapel Union for relief, he (with his family) was admitted to the Union House, kept there 3 weeks & turned out without a farthing in the world to assist him he was compelled to apply again was admitted kept in One week and turned out, starvation compelled him to apply to the Magistrate and the Magistrate forwarded a note to the Relieving Officer requesting him to admit your Petitioner but the Relieving Officer said no he would let the Magistrate see that the Guardians had more authority and Power than the

Magistrate and he would not admit him and your Petitioner declares that had not the Magistrate humanely relieved your Petitioner from the Poor box his family and himself must have Perished

That your Petitioner cannot obtain any employment and he is still refused any assistance from the Parish he legally claims and he and his family are rapidly sinking from starvation. Your Petitioner can if required produce credentials of character from his late employers as to industry honesty & sobriety and your Petitioner trusts that you will be pleased to take this case into your gracious consideration and order him relief from the quarter that your Petitioner thinks has a right to assist him

And your Petitioner

As in duty bound

Shall ever pray

No. 10 Little Pearl
Street Spitalfields
5th July 1847

Source: Public Record Office, [1], MH 12/7916.

DOCUMENT 5   INSUBORDINATE PAUPERS, 1850

The Master of Bethnal Green Workhouse, when asked for his observations on the allegations printed below, informed the Poor Law Board that all were without foundation and that the complainants were troublemakers undergoing punishment for insubordinate conduct.

Bethnal Green Workhouse   Feb. 6, [18]50

To the Commissioners of the Poor Laws

Sirs,

We your humble servants the Inmates of the above workhouse humbly ask your protection from the [sundries] of cruelties practised on us by the Master. We are kept locked in the cell yard to break stones and kept on Bread and Water every other 24 hours because we cannot break 5 bushels of stone per Day being Mechanics and never broke any before the stones being so bad that men that have been used to get their living by breaking them cannot do the task we have been this last three weeks kept on Bread and Water not having any meat but on Sundays have become very weak and most of us having large families and are not allowed a days liberty to look for employment – so that we have the very least chance of taking our familys out the cruelty going on in this place is beyond description it is a disgrace to a christian land boasting of humanity.

Gentlemen we your humble petitioners beg that you will look into our case as soon as you can make it convenient, we are all willing to work and do the best we can and we your petitioners will feel truly thankful

	Their mark
James Shrimpton	X
Edward Mills	X
George Craddock	X
William Sheppard	X
Alexander Cecil	X
George Hanchard	X
Henry Simpson	X
Alfred Humphreys	X

Source: Public Record Office, [1], MH12/6845.

DOCUMENT 6   OUTDOOR RELIEF REGULATION ORDERS, 1852

Note the differences between the orders of August and December. The Instructional Letter, issued with the latter, seems to suggest numerous exploitable loopholes. How these documents were interpreted, though, remains a matter of contention among historians.

(i) August 1852:

... Article 1. Whenever the Guardians shall allow relief to any indigent poor person, out of the Workhouse, *one third* at least of such relief allowed to any person who shall be indigent and helpless from age, sickness, accident, or bodily or mental infirmity, or who shall be a widow having a child or children dependent on her incapable of working, and *one half* at least of the relief allowed to any able-bodied person, other than such widow as aforesaid, shall be given in articles of food or fuel, or in other articles of absolute necessity.

Article 2. In any case in which the Guardians allow relief for longer period than one week to an indigent poor person, without requiring that such person shall be received into the Workhouse, such relief shall be given or administered weekly . . .

(ii) December 1852:

. . . ARTICLE 1. Whenever the Guardians allow relief to any ablebodied male person, out of the workhouse, one half at least of the relief so allowed shall be given in articles of food or fuel, or in other articles of absolute necessity.

ARTICLE 2. In any case in which the Guardians allow relief for a longer period than one week to an indigent poor person, resident within their Union or Parish respectively, without requiring that such person shall be received into the workhouse, such relief shall be given or administered weekly, or at such more frequent periods as they may deem expedient.

ARTICLE 3. It shall not be lawful for the Guardians or their officers —

To establish any applicant for relief in trade or business;

Nor to redeem from pawn for any such applicant any tools, implements, or other articles;

Nor to purchase and give to such applicant any tools, implements, or other articles, except articles of clothing or bedding where urgently needed, and such articles as are herein-before referred to in Art I . . .

Nor to pay, wholly or in part, the rent of the house or lodging of any pauper, nor to apply any portion of the relief ordered to be given to any pauper in payment of any such rent, nor to retain any portion of such relief for the purpose of directly or indirectly discharging such rent, in full or in part, for any such pauper . . .

ARTICLE 5. No relief shall be given to any able-bodied male person while he is employed for wages or other hire or remuneration by any person.

ARTICLE 6. Every able-bodied male person, if relieved out of the workhouse, shall be set to work by the Guardians, and be kept employed under their direction and superintendence so long as he continues to receive relief . . .

(iii) Instructional Letter, December 1852:

. . . Article 5 prohibits the giving relief to able-bodied male paupers while employed for wages. The evils of such a system of relief have been found so great in practice as to be almost universally admitted, and are prominently indicated by the Legislature in the 4 & 5 William 4. cap. 76. s. 52. as forming the principal ground on which the Poor Law Commissioners were by that Act invested with the power and charged with the duty of making regulations for the due administration of relief to able-bodied persons. The Board desire, however, to point out, that what it is intended actually to prohibit is the giving relief at the same identical time as that at which the person receiving it is in actual employment, and in the receipt of wages, (unless he falls within any of the exceptions afterwards set forth), and that relief given in any other case, as, for instance, in that of a man working for wages on one day and being without work the next, or working half the week and being unemployed during the remainder, and being then in need of relief, is not prohibited by this Article.

Article 6 is framed to meet an ordinary state of circumstances, and the Board must remark with satisfaction, that there appears to be nothing in the existing state of things to prevent its being carried into full operation. If, however, owing to any commercial pressure or general depression of trade, large masses of people should hereafter be thrown out of employment, the Board admit that great difficulty would exist in giving full effect to the provisions of the Article. In such an emergency, instances of which have occurred in former years, the Board would, upon the representation of the Guardians, be prepared at once, as on former occasions, to take such steps, by temporary suspension of this Article or otherwise, as might be expedient to meet satisfactorily and effectually the difficulty experienced. As a general rule, however, applicable to all ordinary circumstances, the Board believe that this Article is both practicable and well calculated to aid in securing a due administration of relief to the able-bodied male poor.

Source: Poor Law Board, [5], *Fifth Annual Report*, Appendices 1 & 3 (1852); L(1852–3), pp. 17, 24–6, 28–9.

DOCUMENT 7   A MOTHER'S LETTER, 1857

Although the central authority declined to intervene in individual cases, letters from the poor frequently caused inquiry to be made. The example printed below is accompanied by a minute from Poor Law Inspector H. D. Farrell [dated 16 February 1857] proposing to visit the workhouse 'as soon as I can'.

Bethnal green Workhouse

February 13, 1857

Gentlemen,
    it is right you do cum and see oure children bad for munths with hich

and gets wors the Master nor gardans wont see to it and if we giv oure names we shall get loked up Haste to see all and sum name Sarle and Sisel – soon as you can

A Mother

Source: Public Record Office, [1], MH12/6847.

DOCUMENT 8   AN INMATE'S OBSERVATIONS, 1857

The following letter, which tells us something about the thoughts and feelings of the inmate population, was shown to the Whitechapel guardians for their observations.

February. 10th 1857

To The Poor law Board of Commissioners

Kind Gentlemen of the Board:

I am an old inmate of the Union House situated in Charles Street, Mile End new Town, Whitechapel Union I wish to inform you of the Cruel and Barbarous Treatment inflicted on the inmates of the Union by the Male officer Mr Parkhul [?] the usage is most shameful, on the 26th Day of last Month after Dinner when I came out of the Dining Hall I heard that one of the young Women was kept back by him through some of the others that was either laughing or talking when they were comoing out of the Dining Hall. I went to the Hall door to ask her what was the matter when he seized me by the hands and if it had not been for one of the Inmates draging me away he would have thrown me down the Matron was told of it and i was confinded in the cell all the afternoon till 7 o clock she would not listen to me to know the cause of the disturbance the inmates are not allowed to speak one word in their own behalf but either drove or draged more than a felon or Murderer before him, during the time he has been there he has had more of the Inmates punished in one month than any of the officers has done in three months the sound of his voice strike as a dagger to the Hearts not only to the young but to the old people for they tremble as an aspen leaf at the sight of him the old people are afraid to make any complaint even if they are asked by anyone becaus of losing the liberty of a sunday or Holiday – there are several of the other inmates has been sorely illtreated by him besides me the cells that the Inmates are confined in are in a most fearful condition either from the rain or other damp the boards are as if water was thrown down from wet the poor creatures that has visitors to see them are not permitted to have a bit of tea or jam given them by their friends the sick and dying [ones]? are not even granted that small privilege.

Source: Public Record Office, [1], MH12/7928.

DOCUMENT 9   THE GOSCHEN MINUTE, 1869

George Joachim Goschen (1831–1907) served as president of the Poor Law Board (1868–71) in Gladstone's first administration but later broke from the Liberals over Irish Home Rule in 1886. He twice held office under Lord Salisbury. His minute indicates the shifting balance in the mixed economy of welfare.

THE published statements of Metropolitan pauperism have for some weeks past shown a considerable increase in the number of the out-door poor, not only as compared with previous weeks, but as compared with the high totals of 1867 and 1868. At the same time it has come to the knowledge of the Board that many persons (especially in the East End of London) who two winters ago were most eager in soliciting charitable contributions have now expressed the opinion that the large sums spent then in charity tended to attract pauperism to those districts where money flowed most freely, and that they deprecate a repetition of the system then pursued. Under these circumstances the Board consider it equally important to guard on the one hand against any alarm which might arise on the part of the public, and result in an indiscriminate distribution of charitable funds, and on the other hand to take such precautions and make such preparations as may enable Boards of Guardians and charitable agencies to work with effect and rapidity if any emergency should arise. And, indeed, without considering the question of an increase in the numbers of the out-door poor, and looking simply to the present expenditure on poor relief, it appears to be a matter of essential importance that an attempt should be made to bring the authorities administering the Poor Laws and those who administer charitable funds to as clear an understanding as possible, so as to avoid the double distribution of relief to the same persons, and at the same time to secure that the most effective use should be made of the large sums habitually contributed by the public towards relieving such cases as the Poor Law can scarcely reach.

The question arises, how far it is possible to mark out the separate limits of the Poor Law and of charity respectively, and how it is possible to secure joint action between the two.

One of the most recognized principles in our Poor Law is, that relief should be given only to the actually destitute, and not in aid of wages. In the case of widows with families, where it is often manifestly impossible that the earnings of the woman can support the family, the rule is frequently departed from, but, as a general principle, it lies at the root of the present system of relief. In innumerable cases its application appears to be harsh for the moment, and it might also be held to be an aggravation of an existing difficulty to insist that, so long as a person is in employment, and wages are earned, though such wages may be insufficient, the Poor Law authorities ought to hold aloof and refuse to supplement the receipts of the family, actually offering in preference to take upon themselves the entire cost of their maintenance. Still it is certain that no system could be more dangerous, both to the working classes and to the ratepayers, than to supplement insufficiency of wages by the expenditure of public money.

The fundamental doctrine of the English Poor Laws, in which they differ from those of most other countries, is that relief is given, not as a matter of charity but of legal obligation, and to extend this legal obligation beyond the class to which it now applies, namely, the actually destitute, to a further and much larger class, namely, those in receipt of insufficient wages, would be not only to increase to an unlimited extent the present enormous expenditure, but to allow the belief in a legal claim to public money in every emergency to supplant, in a further portion of the population, the full recognition of the necessity for self-reliance and thrift.

It is clear, therefore, that the Poor Law authorities could not be allowed without public danger to extend their operations beyond those persons who are actually destitute, and for whom they are at present legally bound to provide. It would seem to follow that charitable organizations, whose alms could in no case be claimed as a right, would find their most appropriate sphere in assisting those who have some, but insufficient means, and who, though on the verge of pauperism, are not actual paupers, leaving to the operation of the general law the provision for the totally destitute.

Source: Poor Law Board, [5], *Twenty-Second Annual Report*, Appendix A, No. 4, 1869–70, XXXV, (1870), p. 10.

DOCUMENT 10   THE CRUSADE AGAINST OUTDOOR RELIEF, 1871

Some historians claim to detect a softening in poor law policy in the late-nineteenth century. The following document suggests otherwise.

OUT-DOOR RELIEF.—CIRCULAR from the LOCAL GOVERNMENT BOARD to the POOR LAW INSPECTORS.

Local Government Board, Whitehall, S. W., STR, 2nd December 1871.

THE large increase which has within the last few years taken place in the amount of out-door relief has been regarded by the Local Government Board with much anxiety, and has led them to institute special inquiries in the metropolis, and in the counties of Berks, Cornwall, Devon, Dorset,

Gloucester, Kent, Somerset, Southampton, Surrey, Sussex, and Wilts.

In addition to these inquiries, the Board have, as you are aware, instructed their Inspectors to report upon the state of out-door relief in their several districts.

Many causes have doubtless contributed to the increase in out-door relief which has taken place; but the Board believe, from the information before them, that it is not to any considerable extent attributable to defects in the law or orders which regulate out-door relief. So far, therefore, as the increase is attributable to defective management or administration of the law, the remedy is in the hands of its local administrators, the Guardians, and may be at once applied by them.

The Board trust that you will take as early an opportunity as your engagements will permit, to bring this subject before the several Boards of Guardians in the district under your supervision. Your own knowledge of the circumstances of **particular** Unions will enable you to urge upon Guardians the special suggestions that may be applicable to each Union. But the Board desire to submit to you some facts and considerations that may assist in obtaining considerable general improvement, as well as greater uniformity, in the administration of relief throughout the country.

The cost of out-door relief in England and Wales in the year 1860 amounted to £2,862,753, whilst the out-door relief for the year 1870 amounted to £3,633,051, being an increase of £770,308 . . .

The ratio of out-door paupers to the population was, in 1860, 1 in every 27, and, in 1870, 1 in every 25.

Making every allowance for the increase of population, stagnation in trades, and temporary disturbances in the labour market, variations in the seasons, and other causes which necessarily influence Poor Law relief generally, the increase in the cost of out-door relief is so great, as to excite apprehension; and to suggest that measures should be taken, not only to check any further increase, but to diminish the present amount.

Against all the causes which tend to an increased expenditure of the rates in the form of out-door relief, it is impossible effectually to guard; but it ought to be possible to guard, for the future, against such expenditure as may arise from a too lax or indiscriminate system of administration.

The inquiries which have been made by the Board show conclusively,—

1. That out-door relief is in many cases granted by the Guardians too readily and without sufficient inquiry, and that they give it also in numerous instances in which it would be more judicious to apply the workhouse test, and to adhere more strictly to the provisions of the orders and regulations in force in regard to out-door relief.
2. That there is a great diversity of practice in the administration of out-door relief and that a marked contrast is shown in the numbers relieved, and in the amount of the relief granted in the Unions in which the Guardians adhere strictly to the law, and in those in which they more or less disregard it . . .

3. It has been shown that in numerous instances the Guardians disregard the advantages which result not only to the ratepayers but to the poor themselves from the offer of in-door in preference to out-door relief. A certainty of obtaining outdoor relief in his own home whenever he may ask for it extinguishes in the mind of the labourer all motive for husbanding his resources, and induces him to rely exclusively upon the rates instead of upon his own savings for such relief as he may require. It removes every incentive to self-reliance and prudent forethought on his part, and induces him, moreover, to apply for relief on occasions when the circumstances are not such as to render him absolutely in need of it.

Source: Local Government Board, [6], *First Annual Report*, Appendix A, No. 20, 1871-2, XXVIII, (1872), pp. 63–6.

DOCUMENT 11   MANCHESTER GUARDIANS' REGULATIONS ON OUTDOOR RELIEF, 1875

The 'crusade' against outrelief led to a general tightening of administration which struck with particular harshness at women.

1. Out-door relief shall not be granted or allowed by the Relief Committees, except in case of sickness, to applicants of any of the following classes:—

    (a.) Single able-bodied men.

    (b) Single able-bodied women.

    (c) Able-bodied widows without children, or having only one child to support.

    (d) Married women (with or without families) whose husbands, having been convicted of crime, are undergoing a term of imprisonment.

    (e) Married women (with or without families) deserted by their husbands.

    (f) Married women (with or without families) left destitute through their husbands having joined the militia, and being called up for training.

    (g) Persons residing with relatives, where the united income of the family is sufficient for the support of all its members, whether such relatives are liable by law to support the applicant or not.

2. Out-door relief shall not be granted in any case for a longer period than thirteen weeks at a time.

3. Out-door relief shall not be granted to any able-bodied person for a longer period than six weeks at a time.

4. Out-door relief shall not be granted, on account of the sickness of the applicant, or any of his family, for a longer period than two weeks at a

time, unless such sickness shall be certified in writing by the district medical officer as being likely to be of long duration, or to be of a permanent character.

5. Where relief is allowed to a parent through the admission of a child or children into the Swinton schools or the workhouse, such relief shall not be granted for a longer period than six months at a time; and if at the expiration of such period a continuance of the relief is required, the relieving officer shall visit and inquire into the circumstances of the parent, and bring the case up for re-consideration by the Relief Committee, in the same manner as if it were a case of out-door relief.

Source: Local Government Board, [6], *Fifth Annual Report*, Appendix B, No.188, 1875–76, XXXI, (1876), p. 133.

DOCUMENT 12   **TERROR IN MILE END, 1886**

The Whitechapel Workhouse was upheld as a model establishment by the Charity Organization Society. Its rigorous use of the labour test was deemed admirable. Inmates held a different view of its alleged progressive character.

Mile End Old Town

To The Medical Officer,
Local Government Board
[Stamped 8 January 1886]

Sir,

I beg to call your attention to the cruelty exercised by the master and the Mile End Board of Guardians in sending a portion of their aged and infirm poor to the Whitechapel Test House, South Grove. The Master (Mr Waterer) said publicly: – 'The rules and regulations of this House are necessarily very severe. I should like to make some distinction, but I cannot; all must be treated alike.' Now, if the Master acknowledges the treatment to be *very severe*, I leave you to judge if it is a propert place to send aged men, between 60 and 75 to, especially as most of them have some complaint which prevents them from following any of their usual avocations. Most of those sent there within the last two years have been sent to the infirmary, either to die, or to remain living specimens of this cruel treatment. I will only add, that such is the terror created at Mile End from the account given by those who have been sent there, that they are afraid to make the slightest complaint about anything, knowing that penal servitude at South Grove would be the consequence. Should a return be demanded of all the men over 60 that have been sent there from Mile End within the last two years, I think the death rate would cause some astonishment.

I am, Sir, your obdt Servant.

One of the Victims.

Source: Public Record Office, [1], MH12/7546.

DOCUMENT 13   THE CHAMBERLAIN CIRCULAR, 1886

Joseph Chamberlain (1836–1914), served as Lord Mayor of Birmingham from 1873 to 1876 and entered Parliament as an energetic social reformer. His radicalism and its limitations are evident in his response to the mass unemployment of the 1880s.

Pauperism and Distress: Circular Letter to Boards of Guardians

Local Government Board, Whitehall, S. W.

15th March 1886

Sir,
    The enquiries which have been recently undertaken by the Local Government Board unfortunately confirm the prevailing impression as to the existence of exceptional distress amongst the working classes. This distress is partial as to its locality, and is no doubt due in some measure to the long continued severity of the weather.
    The returns of pauperism show an increase, but it is not yet considerable; and the numbers of persons in receipt of relief are greatly below those of previous periods of exceptional distress.
    The Local Government Board have, however, thought it their duty to go beyond the returns of actual pauperism which are all that come under their notice in ordinary times, and they have made some investigation into the condition of the working classes generally.
    They are convinced that in the ranks of those who do not ordinarily seek poor law relief there is evidence of much and increasing privation, and if the depression in trade continues it is to be feared that large numbers of persons usually in regular employment will be reduced to the greatest straits.
    Such a condition of things is a subject for deep regret and very serious consideration.
    The spirit of independence which leads so many of the working classes to make great personal sacrifices rather than incur the stigma of pauperism, is

one which deserves the greatest sympathy and respect, and which it is the duty and interest of the community to maintain by all the means at its disposal.

Any relaxation of the general rule at present obtaining, which requires as a condition of relief to able-bodied male persons on the ground of their being out of employment, the acceptance of an order for admission to the workhouse, or the performance of an adequate task of work as a labour test, would be most disastrous, tending directly to restore the condition of things which, before the reform of poor laws destroyed the independence of the labouring classes and increased the poor rate until it became an almost unsupportable burden.

It is not desirable that the working classes should familiarised with poor law relief, and if once the honourable sentiment which now leads them to avoid it is broken down, it is probable that recourse will be had to this provision on the slightest occasion ... What is required in the endeavour to relieve artisans and others who have hitherto avoided poor law assistance, and who are temporarily deprived of employment is:

1. Work which will not involve the stigma of pauperism;
2. Work which all can perform, whatever may have been their previous avocations;
3. Work which does not compete with that of other labourers at present in employment;

And, lastly, work which is not likely to interfere with resumption of regular employment in their own trades by those who seek it.

The Board have no power to enforce the adoption of any particular proposals, and the object of this circular is to bring the subject generally under the notice of boards of guardians and other local authorities.

In districts in which exceptional distress prevails, the Board recommend that the guardians should confer with the local authorities, and endeavour to arrange with the latter for the execution of works on which unskilled labour may be immediately employed.

These works may be of the following kinds, among others:

(a) Spade husbandry on sewage farms;
(b) Laying out of open spaces, recreation grounds, cemeteries, or disused burial grounds;
(c) Cleansing of streets not usually undertaken by local authorities;
(d) Laying out and paving of new streets, etc.;
(e) Paving of unpaved streets, and making of footpaths in country roads;
(f) Providing or extending sewerage works and works of water supply.

It may be observed, that spade labour is a class of work which has special advantages in the case of able-bodied persons out of employment. Every ablebodied man can dig, although some can do more than others, and it is work which is in no way degrading, and need not interfere with existing employment.

In all cases in which special works are undertaken to meet exceptional distress, it would appear to be necessary, 1st, that the men employed should be engaged on the recommendation of the guardians as persons whom, owing to previous condition and circumstances, it is undesirable to send to the workhouse, or to treat as subjects for pauper relief, and 2nd that the wages paid should be something less than the wages ordinarily paid for similar work, in order to prevent imposture, and to leave the strongest temptations to those who avail themselves of this opportunity to return as soon as possible to their previous occupations.

When the works are of such a character that the expenses may properly be defrayed out of borrowed moneys, the local authorities may rely that there will be every desire on the part of the Board to deal promptly with the application for their sanction to a loan.

I shall be much obliged if you will keep me informed of the state of affairs in your district, and if it should be found necessary to make any exceptional provision, I shall be glad to know at once the nature of such provision, and the extent to which those for whom it is intended avail themselves of it.

I am, etc.,

(Signed) J. Chamberlain

Source: Local Government Board, [6], *Sixteenth Annual Report*, 1886–7, XXXVI, (1887), pp. 5–7.

DOCUMENT 14   BECOMING A GUARDIAN, 1894

In the following extract a member of the Women's Co-operative Guild recalls the deterrent attitudes encountered by women who sought to participate in poor law administration.

I was first asked to become a candidate for the Board of Guardians previous to the property qualification being done away with, but declined. When the Act of 1894 was passed I consented to stand, and won a contested election. Twice since then, at the termination of three years' office, I have been returned without opposition.

The Vicar of the Parish opposed my nomination the first time, but on the last occasion of election, the Churchwarden sent me my nomination paper filled up, without any solicitation, showing some prejudice overcome.

The Chairman of the Board, January 1895, told the women members privately that he was much against women coming there (we were then elected but had not taken our seats), he kindly inviting us to an interview in the Board Room to make our acquaintance and explain some of our duties. He would be like the boy with the physic, he said, make the best of it. He thought we should be useful to see that the children's heads were kept clean, etc. Then he was anxious to know if we should wish to sit when speaking at the Board, as if we did, some men would too, and it was difficult enough to keep order now . . .

The interview continued: 'Where should we sit?' That chair was so and so's, and this ditto, and Mr. – would not know himself if he did not have his corner – he was sure we did not wish to inconvenience any of the old fossils . . .

Then when it was first proposed to send women to Poor Law Conferences, a cry was raised at the Board, 'Let the women stay at home and cook their husbands' dinners.' Since then for three years in succession I have been elected as one of two representatives to the Central Poor Law Conference.

Another of our Women Guardians had worked for years at office cleaning from 5 a.m. to breakfast time, and helped to maintain her widowed mother . . .

Source: M. Llewellyn Davies, [12], pp. 129–31.

DOCUMENT 15   THE CAUSES OF PAUPERISM: EVIDENCE
FROM EAST LONDON, 1889

Charles Booth's poverty studies included a detailed analysis of the Stepney Union. The following particulars, taken from the relieving officer's casebook, were used by Booth to illustrate the need for non-contributory old age pensions.
Principal Causes of Pauperism at Stepney (by Institutions).

Principal or Obvious Causes.	Poplar, Able-bodied		Bromley, Infirm.		Sick Asylum		Summary.				Contributory Causes.			
	Number	Per Cent.	Number	Per Cent.	Number	Per Cent.	Males.	Females.	Total.	Per Cent.	Drink.	Pauper Association and Heredity.	Sickness.	Old Age.
Drink	10	19.6	50	11.3	20	14.2	53	27	80	12.6	—	23	11	11
Immorality	7	13.7	5	1.1	4	2.9	6	10	16	2.5	3	3	3	1
Laziness	3	5.8	6	1.4	3	2.1	10	2	12	1.9	6	5	1	3
Pauper association and heredity	1	2.0	4	0.9	2	1.4	6	1	7	1.1	1	—	2	2
Incapacity, temper, etc	5	9.8	19	4.3	—	—	17	7	24	3.8	4	5	2	6
Extravagance..	—	—	8	1.8	—	—	7	1	8	1.3	4	2	—	3
Lack of work or trade misfortune	3	9.8	23	5.2	—	—	26	2	28	4.4	4	—	5	13
Accident	—	—	25	5.7	5	3.5	25	5	30	4.7	4	2	1	14
Death of husband	4	7.9	20	4.5	2	1.4	—	26	26	4.1	3	2	10	8
Desertion	1	2.0	2	0.5	—	—	—	3	3	0.5	3	—	1	1
Mental derangement	3	5.8	7	1.6	1	0.7	3	8	11	1.7	1	2	—	2
Sickness	8	15.7	76	17.2	85	60.3	98	71	169	26.7	24	38	5	41
Old age	—	—	192	43.4	16	11.4	113	95	208	32.8	22	18	44	—
Other causes ..	4	7.9	5	1.1	3	2.1	9	3	12	1.9	6	6	2	2
	51	100.0	442	100.0	141	100.0	373	261	634	100.0	85	106	87	107
Children	2	—	21	—	13	—	22	14	36	—	—	—	—	—
Old cases, no record	—	—	41	—	1	—	20	22	42	—	—	—	—	—
	53	—	504	—	155	—	415	297	712	—	—	—	—	—

Source: C. Booth, [10, Industry Series, Vol. 4], p. 314.

DOCUMENT 16   ROYAL COMMISSION ON POOR LAWS
AND RELIEF OF DISTRESS, THE
MAJORITY REPORT, 1909

*The prominence given to organized voluntary charity in a new scheme of
public welfare was the central feature of the Majority Report which,
without seeking to defend the principles of 1834, gave full expression to the
radicalism of the Charity Organization Society.*

(38). CONCLUSION.

167.   The proposals we make cover a large field of administration, will
conflict with many old traditions, and will take time before they can come
into really effective operation. But the evils we have had to describe are so
widespread and deeprooted, and form so integral a part of the social life of
the country, that no remedies less in scope or in force would in our
judgment be sufficient.

168.   But great as are the administrative changes which we propose, and
costly as some of the new establishments may be, we feel strongly that the
pauperism and distress we have described can never be successfully
combatted by administration and expenditure. The causes of distress are not
only economic and industrial; in their origin and character they are largely
moral. Government by itself cannot correct or remove such influences.
Something more is required. The co-operation, spontaneous and whole-
hearted, of the community at large, and especially of those sections of it
which are well to-do and free from the pressure of poverty, is indispensable.
There is evidence from many quarters to show that the weak part of our
system is not want of public spirit or benevolence, or lack of funds or of
social workers, or of the material out of which these can be made. Its
weakness is lack of organisation, of method, and of confidence in those who
administer the system. We have so framed the new system as to invite and
bring into positions of authority the best talent and experience that the
locality can provide. In addition to those vested with such authority we
have left a place in the new system for all capable and willing social
workers; but they must work in accord, under guidance, and in the sphere
allotted to them.

169.   Great Britain is the home of voluntary effort, and its triumphs and
successes constitute in themselves much of the history of the country. But
voluntary effort when attacking a common and ubiquitous evil must be
disciplined and led. We have here to learn a lesson from foreign countries
whose charitable and social organisations, notably in France, Germany,
Belgium, and Holland, work under ˙ official guidance with efficacy,
promptitude, and success. Looking at the voluntary resources and societies
at our disposal there is every reason to believe that we can vie with and

surpass any results obtained abroad. To this end it is organisation we need, and this organisation we now suggest.

173.   'Land of Hope and Glory' is a popular and patriotic lyric sung each year with rapture by thousands of voices. The enthusiasm is partly evoked by the beauty of the idea itself, but more by the belief that Great Britain does, above other countries, merit this eulogium, and that the conditions in existence here are such that the fulfilment of hope and the achievement of glory are more open to the individual than in other and less favoured lands. To certain classes of the community into whose moral and material condition it has been our duty to enquire, these words are a mockery and a falsehood. To many of them, possibly from their own failure and faults, there is in this life but little hope, and to many more 'glory' or its realisation is an unknown ideal. Our investigations prove the existence in our midst of a class whose condition and environment are a discredit, and a peril to the whole community. Each and every section of society has a common duty to perform in combating this evil and contracting its area, a duty which can only be performed by united and untiring effort to convert useless and costly inefficients into self-sustaining and respectable members of the community. No country, however rich, can permanently hold its own in the race of international competition, if hampered by an increasing load of this dead weight; or can successfully perform the role of sovereignty beyond the seas, if a portion of its own folk at home are sinking below the civilization and aspirations of its subject races abroad.

Source: Royal Commission on the Poor Laws and the Relief of Distress, [9], *Majority Report* (Cd 4499), XXXVII, Part IX, 1909, pp. 643–4.

DOCUMENT 17   ROYAL COMMISSION ON THE POOR LAWS AND RELIEF OF DISTRESS, THE MINORITY REPORT, 1909

The Minority Report saw poverty arising from the organisation of the economy; and whereas the Majority sought to reconstruct the Poor Law, the Minority assumed that progress in social policy waited upon its total abolition.

THE SCHEME OF REFORM.

The state of anarchy and confusion, into which has fallen the whole realm of relief and assistance to the poor and to persons in distress, is so generally recognised that many plans of reform have been submitted to us, each representing a section of public opinion. In fact, throughout the three years of our investigations we have been living under a continuous pressure for a remodelling of the Poor Laws and the Unemployed Workmen Act, in one direction or another. We do not regret this peremptory and insistent demand for reform. The present position is, in our opinion, as grave as that of 1834, though in its own way. We have, on the one hand, in England and Wales, Scotland and Ireland alike, the well-established Destitution Authorities, under ineffective central control, each pursuing its own policy in its own way; sometimes rigidly restricting its relief to persons actually destitute, and giving it in the most deterrent and humiliating forms; sometimes launching out into an indiscriminate and unconditional subsidising of mere poverty; sometimes developing costly and palatial institutions for the treatment, either gratuitously or for partial payment, of practically any applicant of the wage-earning or of the lower middle class. On the other hand, we see existing, equally ubiquitous with the Destitution Authorities, the newer specialised organs of Local Government – the Local Education Authority, the Local Health Authority, the Local Lunacy Authority, the Local Unemployment Authority, the Local Pension Authority – all attempting to provide for the needs of the poor, *according to the cause or character of their distress*. Every Parliamentary session adds to the powers of these specialised Local Authorities. Every Royal Commission or Departmental Committee recommends some fresh development of their activities ... Athwart the overlapping and rivalry of these half a dozen Local Authorities that may be all at work in a single district, we watch the growing stream of private charity and voluntary agencies – almshouses and pensions for the aged; hospitals and dispensaries, convalescent homes and 'medical missions' for the sick; free dinners and free boots, country holidays and 'happy evenings' for the children; free shelters and soup kitchens, 'way tickets' and charitable jobs for the able-bodied, together with uncounted indiscriminate doles of every description – without systematic organisation and without any co-ordination with the multifarious forms of public activity. What the nation is confronted with to-day is, as it was in 1834, an ever-growing expenditure from public and private funds, which results, on the one hand, in a minimum of prevention and cure, and on the other in far-reaching demoralisation of character and the continuance of no small amount of unrelieved destitution.

Deferring our proposals with regard to the whole of the Able-bodied until Part II. of the present Report, we recommend:—

90.   That, except the 43 Eliz., c.2, the Poor Law Amendment Act of 1834 for England and Wales and the various Acts for the relief of the poor and the corresponding legislation for Scotland and Ireland, so far as they relate exclusively to Poor Relief, and including the Law of Settlement, should be repealed.

91.   That the Boards of Guardians in England, Wales and Ireland, and (at any rate as far as Poor Law functions are concerned) the Parish Councils in Scotland, together with all combinations of these bodies, should be abolished.

92. That the property and liabilities, powers and duties of these Destitution Authorities should be transferred (subject to the necessary adjustments) to the County and County Borough Councils, strengthened in numbers as may be deemed necessary for their enlarged duties; with suitable modifications to provide for the special circumstances of Scotland and Ireland, and for the cases of the Metropolitan Boroughs, the Non-County Boroughs over 10,000 in population, and the Urban Districts over 20,000 in population, on the plan that we have sketched out.

93. That the provision for the various classes of the nonable-bodied should be wholly separated from that to be made for the Able-bodied, whether these be Unemployed workmen, vagrants or able-bodied persons now in receipt of Poor Relief.

94. That the services at present administered by the Destitution Authorities (other than those connected with vagrants or the able-bodied) – that is to say, the provision for:—

  (i) Children of school age;
  (ii) The sick and the permanently incapacitated, the infants under school age, and the aged needing institutional care;
  (iii) The mentally defective of all grades and all ages; and
  (iv) The aged to whom pensions are awarded – should be assumed, under the directions of the County and County Borough Councils, by:— (i) The Education Committee; (ii) The Health Committee; (iii) The Asylums Committee; and (iv) The Pension Committee respectively.

95. That the several committees concerned should be authorised and required under the directions of their Councils, to provide, under suitable conditions and safeguards to be embodied in Statutes and regulative Orders, for the several classes of persons committed to their charge, whatever treatment they may deem most appropriate to their condition; being either institutional treatment, in the various specialised schools, hospitals, asylums, etc., under their charge; or whenever judged preferable, domiciliary treatment, conjoined with the grant of Home Ailment where this is indispensably required.

96. That the law with regard to liability to pay for relief or treatment received, or to contribute towards the maintenance of dependents and other relations, should be embodied in a definite and consistent code, on the basis, in those services for which a charge should be made, of recovering the cost from all those who are really able to pay, and of exempting those who cannot properly do so.

97. That there should be established in each County and County Borough one or more officers, to be designated Registrars of Public

Assistance, to be appointed by the County and County Borough Council, and to be charged with the threefold duty of:—

(i) Keeping a Public Register of all cases in receipt of public assistance;
(ii) Assessing and recovering, according to the law of the land and the evidence as to sufficiency of ability to pay, whatever charges Parliament may decide to make for particular kinds of relief or treatment; and
(iii) Sanctioning the Grants of Home Ailment proposed by the Committees concerned with the treatment of the case.

98.   That the Registrar of Public Assistance should have under his direction (and under the control of the General Purposes Committee of the County or County Borough Council) the necessary staff of Inquiry and Recovery Officers, and a local Receiving House, for the strictly temporary accommodation of non-able-bodied persons found in need, and not as yet dealt with by the Committees concerned . . .

PART II.—THE DESTITUTION OF THE ABLE-BODIED.

. . . That the duty of so organising the National Labour Market as to prevent or to minimise Unemployment should be placed upon a Minister responsible to Parliament, who might be designated the Minister for Labour.

Source: Royal Commission on the Poor Laws and the Relief of Distress, [9], *Minority Report* (Cd 4499), XXXVII, Chapter XII, 1909, pp. 999, 1031–2, 1215.

GLOSSARY

able-bodied no formal definition was included in the regulations made under the Poor Law and the term seems capable of several meanings. The Poor Law Amendment Act of 1834 and the Outdoor Relief Prohibitory Order of 1844 focused on the capacity to obtain employment for hire at any wages, whatever the state of health of the worker. In respect of the workhouse, it appears to denote all persons not being either children, the aged and infirm, or the sick.

Benthamism/Benthamite adjective derived from thought of Jeremy Bentham (1748–1832). The prophet of Philosophical Radicalism, he has been credited with what the Webbs described as 'the insidiously potent conception' of a seriers of specialized government departments supervising and controlling from Whitehall, through salaried officials, the whole public administration of the community. As one of the most influential exponents of Utilitarianism, Bentham maintained that social organization had to be adjusted in such a way as to maximize human happiness. Bentham believed that the object of government, as the Webbs put it, 'was to play on the wills of men as if these were a keyboard, in order to harmonize the necessarily conflicting interests of individuals among themselves, and also those of individuals and the community' [25 p. 27]. Bentham's proposal for a Ministry of Indigence influenced close associates like Edwin Chadwick and bore many similarities with the centralized structure of the New Poor Law of 1834.

casual poor term defined by the Poor Law Commission in 1837 as denoting 'wayfarers' or homeless 'persons in a state of destitution ... who ... belonged to distinct parishes'. More usually used by modern historians with reference to the mass of irregularly and underemployed workers who made up much of the labour force in town and country.

Classical economics/economists school of political economists founded by Adam Smith and developed by David Ricardo (1772–1823) and John Stuart Mill (1806–1873) which emphasized the superiority of free private initiative and vigorous competition over government control and regulation of the economy. They believed that the production, consumption and distribution of wealth were determined by economic 'laws' and that the power of competition alone (the 'invisible hand' of the market) determined prices, wages, profits and rent.

Collectivism a term that refers to any political or socioeconomic theory or practice that promotes or fosters the communal or state ownership and control of the means of production and distribution. Collectivism proceeds from the assumption that the pursuit of individual self-interest within an unregulated market tends to produce economic inefficiencies and a social divisiveness that is harmful to the commonweal. Collectivist ideologists have assumed many different forms. These include socialism, marxism, co-operation as well as a range of non-doctrinal practices by which the regulatory and protective functions of the state were extended in the course of the nineteenth century. Benthamism thus combined individual with collectivism. Collectivism is sometimes used erroneously as a shorthand for socialism.

Condition of England Question a term from the 1840s that encapsulated middle-class anxieties in respect of the social tensions released by industrialism, urbanism and the growth of class antagonisms.

Gilbert's Act, 1782 provided for the incorporation of parishes into unions without special legislation; on the eve of the New Poor Law some 900 parishes had come together to form 67 unions with paid relieving officers and a willingness to experiment with outdoor relief.

gruel a thin oatmeal porridge, made only with water and without milk or sugar.

Idealism the philosophical theory that the only things which really exist are ideas – in the Spirit, God or in the minds of individuals – and that the correct way to understand society is through the examination of this thinking. From the 1870s not only were the writings of Kant, Hegel and other German philosophers studied in British universities, but also the Idealist philosophy of the Greeks, especially Plato with its claims for the priority of state and society over the individual and its insistence upon the pursuit of the public good as the object of human association. At Oxford, T.H. Green (1836–1882) taught that social progress could be attained through voluntary co-operation among people rather than through intervention by the state. Nevertheless, Idealism could lead contemporaries in diametrically opposite directions with respect to the desirability of public action. Some, for example, saw non-contributory old age pensions and income tax as crucial to the realization of the public good while others, like the Bosanquets, saw such intervention as its very negation. Some Idealists thought that an individualized casework approach offered the best alleviation of poverty; others preferred a community-orientated approach. In this, as in most areas of social theory, labels need to be affixed with exceptional care.

moral economy term used by historians to denote pre-industrial social and economic order in which workshop and household production were motivated by customary, rather than free-market, notions of economic activity. Artisans and employers were committed to traditional needs and practices, to the idea of a 'sufficiency' obtained by means of 'fair' wages, 'just' prices, 'honest' profits and 'honourable' masters rather than the maximizing imperatives of the unregulated market. Upholders of the 'moral economy' sought to control and regulate the market by custom and law so as to protect labour in relation to consumption and production, to preserve the social and economic fabric of the community and to forestall the development of 'dishonourable' employers and 'dishonourable' free-market practices. These customary notions came under pressure by the rapid growth of commodity production bringing the introduction of capitalist practices into work organization and work relationships and capitalist values into conventional understandings of duty and social obligation.

Nineteenth-century revolution in government a contested term to describe the process of self-generating administrative growth that is said to have been characteristic of the state in Victorian Britain. It was a response to the demands created by rapid industrial and economic change, *ad hoc* in character and carried forward by its own momentum. The place of Benthamism in all of this has been much debated [121, 126, 135, 147].

Panopticon project for prison reform created by Jeremy Bentham which included provision for a circular type of prison structure which would enable a single warden to survey from the centre all the inmates at any time. Prisoners, aware that they were under constant scrutiny, would behave as required. The possibilities of a control-and-command-style environment may well have influenced workhouse architecture.

Political Economy the theoretical science of the laws of production and distribution; it was based on abstract deductive procedures and was projected by its practitioners as a guide to the management of people and resources and for this reason was exceptionally influential in respect of poor law policy. The self-imposed task of political economy was concerned with examining the processes whereby nature's finite resources were allocated among the various classes of society and the operation of the various factors that set limits to wealth and productivity.

Positivism a social theory associated with the Frenchman Auguste Comte (1798–1857). This was developed in his *Cours de philosophe positive* (1830–42) and in his *Systeme de politique positive* (1861–64). He maintained that human knowledge had evolved in three stages – theological, metaphysical and positive. Positivism, the highest phase, superseded all others. Positivism proposed a religion of humanity which would be dedicated to the improvement of the social conditions of all members of the human race. It provided a secular substitute for those of unsettled faith and was particularly influential among the intelligentsia of mid-Victorian Britain. Its adherents ranged from the novelist George Eliot (1819–1880) to the social reformer Charles Booth.

Rebecca Riots, 1843–44 a crusade against toll gates that occurred in Wales. It was directed principally at turnpike gates and to a lesser extent against workhouses and was organized by the Children of Rebecca. So called from Rebecca, the bride of Isaac. When she left home her father and friends said to her, 'Let thy seed possess the gate of those which hate thee' (Genesis: XXIV, 60).

School Board Visitor school attendance officer.

Sephardi (plural Sephardim) Jews originating from Spain and Portugal at the close of the fifteenth century having a distinctive rite and pronunciation of Hebrew.

Utilitarians/Utilitarianism a system of moral philosophy, also known as Benthamism or Philosophical Radicalism. It exercised a major influence on British political, social, economic and legal thought during the nineteenth century. It took as its starting-point the assumption that the ultimate good lay in the greatest happiness of the greatest number; it defined the rightness of actions in terms of their contribution to the general happiness. Utilitarians believed that their philosophy provided a scientific standard of utility by which to measure the performance of political and legal institutions.

Vagrancy Act 1824 prohibited sleeping in the open and begging in the streets and forced many destitute persons into the casual wards to avoid police action.

wages fund theory scarcity of wealth was one of the basic presuppositions of political economy which posited the existence of a fixed fund for wages in any given year. No agitation on the part of the workers for a greater share could alter this apparent fact of life. Its fallacies were exposed by W.T. Thornton in 1869 and unreservedly abandoned by John Stuart Mill thereafter. It was replaced by a theory of distribution in which the impossibility of a general rise in wages is not even presumed.

women guardians their election was made possible by the removal of discriminatory rating qualifications by the Local Government Act of 1894 in consequence of which their numbers increased from a mere 50 in 1885 to 839 in 1895 and rose thereafter from 1141 in 1907 to 1289 in 1909, mainly in urban areas.

GUIDE TO MAIN CHARACTERS

BARNETT, HENRIETTA (1851–1936), social reformer and founder of Hampstead Garden Suburb. Born Henrietta Rowland into a modestly prosperous family, she became involved with social work with Octavia Hill in Marylebone. After marriage to Samuel Barnet, she became a Poor Law Guardian and noted campaigner for the reform of pauper education. The Hampstead Garden Suburb project as she originally conceived it was intended to bridge the gap between poverty and privilege with provision for young and old and community service.

BARNETT, SAMUEL (1844–1913), a clergyman and social reformer and first warden of Toynbee Hall, East London. He was born in Bristol and educated at Wadham College, Oxford. He was presented to St Judes, Whitechapel in 1873 where he became convinced that the solution to the social problem lay with the restoration of an active benevolence on the part of the privileged classes. In 1884 he founded Toynbee Hall as the first university settlement where Oxbridge graduates could come and live and give practical assistance to those of an inferior station. He was also active in education and poor law reform.

BOSANQUET, HELEN (1850–1925), social theorist and philanthropist. She was born Helen Dendy into a Manchester Unitarian manufacturing family. Her father's business was unsuccessful and she and her siblings had to support themselves. After a spell as a housekeeper she went to Newnham College, Cambridge as a mature student and completed the Moral Sciences Tripos in 1889. Thereafter she worked as a paid secretary for the Shoreditch branch of the Charity Organization Society. She wrote for the *Charity Organization Review* and for the periodical press. In 1895 she married the Idealist philosopher, Bernard Bosanquet. She published a number of important studies of poverty and the poor which were widely used for the training of social workers in the early twentieth century. In them she advocated the importance of individual and personal casework to support the family as the primary unit of society. She was opposed to state intervention. She served as editor of the *Charity Organization Review* from 1908–21. In 1905 she was appointed to the Royal Commission of the Poor Laws and Relief of Distress in which she became the chief advocate of organized voluntary action as expressed in the Majority Report of which she was the chief author.

CHADWICK, EDWIN (1801–1890), civil servant and social reformer. The son of a failed businessman turned journalist, he was called to the bar at Inner Temple in 1830. In the previous year he had published an article on preventative police which secured him the friendship of Jeremy Bentham. He served as Assistant Commissioner to the Royal Commission on the Poor Laws in 1832 and in 1833 was appointed secretary to the commission, the report of which he co-authored with Nassau Senior. He was also a member of the Royal Commission to investigate the condition of factory children in 1833, and served on the Royal Commission on the Constabulary drafting its famous report of 1839. His interests embraced public health as well as public order. He was the author of the *Report on the Sanitary Condition of the Labouring Population of Great Britain* (1842) which was not only a landmark in the campaign for public health improvement but also a significant addition to the literature of empirical social enquiry. As secretary to the Poor Law Commission, 1834–47, he was involved in the implementation of the New Poor Law and as a member of the Board of Health, 1848–54, he made a considerable contribution to the movement for sanitary reform. He was knighted in 1889.

COLLET, CLARA (1860–1948), civil servant and feminist. She was born into a middle-class family of modest means. She attended North London Collegiate School and graduated from University College, London in 1880 of which she became the first woman fellow in 1896. She taught in Leicester schools for some years before joining Charles Booth's Life and Labour Inquiry to which she contributed an important essay on domestic work. With Booth's support she became an Assistant Commissioner on the Royal Commission on Labour and in 1893 secured a permanent post in the Labour Department of the Board of Trade, becoming

Senior Investigator for Women's Industries. She retired in 1920. Thereafter she became an active member of the Royal Economic Society and the Royal Statistical Society. Her numerous writings on women's work are now recognized as an important contribution to an emergent feminist sociology.

COLQUHOUN, PATRICK (1745–1820), social reformer. He was born in Dumbarton, son of a minor official, and made a fortune in Virginia before returning to Glasgow where he served as Lord Provost in 1782 and 1783. He subsequently settled in London where he became a magistrate and noted police reformer. His plans for a centralized poor law authority were similar to those of his friend Jeremy Bentham.

KEMPTHORNE, SAMPSON (1809–1873), architect. He was born in Gloucester and studied at the Royal Academy Schools after which he travelled in Italy as assistant to Sir Gilbert Scott. He set up practice in London and was appointed architect to the Poor Law Commission in 1835. He prepared numerous designs for schools and also designed and built many workhouses in various parts of the country. He went to New Zealand on behalf of the Church Missionary Society in 1842 and remained there in practice in Aukland.

SIMS, G. R. (1847–1922), campaigning journalist. He entered journalism after a spell in the family cabinet-making business and achieved recognition for the rhyming ballads included in his regular column for the *Sunday Referee*. These, when collected and reprinted, became a best-seller. Most famous of them all was *In the Workhouse: Christmas Day* which first appeared in 1877. His exposure of poverty and bad housing, published as *How The Poor Live* (1883), played an important role in stimulating public debate about the social problem.

SMITH, ADAM (1723–1790), Scottish economist; he attended the universities of Glasgow and Oxford and from 1752 held the chair in moral philosophy in Glasgow. His most famous work, *The Wealth of Nations* (1776), is a cogent and engaging account of the socially progressive character of the free market which became a foundational text of political economy and the modern discipline of economics.

TWINING, LOUISA (1820–1912), poor law reformer and feminist. She was born in London, the daughter of a prosperous tea manufacturer. She was drawn into a wide range of philanthropic and charitable activity in the 1840s and was an enthusiastic member of the National Association for the Promotion of Social Science. In 1858 she became secretary of the Workhouse Visiting Society and from 1884–90 served as a Poor Law Guardian in Kensington. She was also President of the Women's Local Government Society and an active member of the suffrage movement. Her ideas and interests are well described in her autobiography *Recollections of Life and Work* (1895). Of interest, too, are her writings on poor law reform including *Workhouses and Women's Work* (1858) and *Workhouses and Pauperism* (1898).

WEBB, BEATRICE (1858–1943), Fabian socialist, diarist, student of society and public-spirited worker. She was born Martha Beatrice Potter, one of ten daughters of the wealthy industrialist Richard Potter. Self-educated, she proceeded from philanthropic activity under the Charity Organization Society to participate in the management of Katharine Buildings, East Smithfield before joining Charles Booth's research team in 1886. Her emotional attachment to Joseph Chamberlain was not returned by the leader of Liberal radicalism and she married Sidney Webb in 1892. Their union, which was initially intellectual and later, apparently, sexual, gave rise to an original and productive partnership which did much to stimulate the development of empirical social inquiry in Britain. She was prominent in public life as a socialist and broadcaster. The first volume of her autobiography *My Apprenticeship* (1926) is a classic account of a Victorian upbringing coupled with a compelling narrative of her development as a social scientist.

WEBB, SIDNEY (1859–1947), socialist theorist and politician. He was born in London into a lower-middle-class family and was educated on the Continent, at Birkbeck College, London and at the City of London College. He entered the civil service in 1878 and was called to the bar in 1885 and took the LL.B. of London University the following year. He joined the Fabian Society in 1885. Beatrice Potter, who became his wife in 1892, described him as 'a remarkable little man with a huge head and a tiny body, a breadth of forehead quite sufficient to account for the encyclopaedic character of his knowledge'. Their working partnership resulted in several classic studies which included *The History of Trade Unionism* (1894), *Industrial Democracy* (1897), and *English Local Government* 9 vols (1906–29). Together they launched the London School of Economics in 1895, drafted the Minority Report of the Royal Commission on the Poor Laws and Relief of Distress in 1909, organized a national campaign in its favour in 1910, founded the *New Statesman* in 1913 and became important Labour Party activists. Sidney served as Labour MP for Seaham, Durham between 1922–29. As a Cabinet Minister in Macdonald's administrations he held office as President of the Board of Trade and Colonial Secretary. In 1929 he was created Baron Passfield. Beatrice refused to use the title. Their impressions of a visit to Russia in 1932 were published as *Soviet Communism: A New Civilization?* in two volumes in 1935. He and Beatrice were buried in Westminster Abbey.

BIBLIOGRAPHY

The place of publication is London unless otherwise stated.

PRIMARY SOURCES: MANUSCRIPT

1 Public Record Office, MH/12 Poor Law Union Papers.
2 Public Record Office, Mepo.3/140, Whitechapel Murders, 1888.
3 University of London Library and British Library of Political and
   Economic Science, Charles Booth Papers.

PRIMARY SOURCES: PRINTED

Official Publications

4 Annual Reports of the Poor Law Commission, 1835–1848.
5 Annual Reports of the Poor Law Board, 1849–1870.
6 Annual Reports of the Local Government Board, 1871–1914.
7 Checkland, S. G. and Checkland, E. O. A., *The 1834 Poor Law
   Report*, Penguin, Harmondsworth, 1974.
8 Glen, W. C., *General Orders of the Poor Law Commissioners*, 1852.
9 Royal Commission on the Poor Laws and the Relief of Distress,
   Majority and Minority Reports XXXVIII, 1909.

Contemporary Works

10 Booth, C., *Life and Labour of the People in London*, 17 vols,
    1902–03.
11 Colquhoun, P., *Treatise on Indigence*, 1806.
12 Davies, M. Llewellyn (ed.), *Life as We Have Known It*, Hogarth
    Press, 1931.
13 Malthus, T.R., *An Essay on the Principles of Population*, 1798.
14 Mayhew, H., *London Labour and the London Poor*, 4 vols, 1862.
15 Rose, M.E., *The English Poor Law 1780–1930*, Sources for Social
    and Economic History, David & Charles, Newton Abbot, 1971.
16 Rowntree, B.S., *Poverty, A Study of Town Life*, Macmillan, 1901.
16a Young, A., *The Farmer's Tour through the East of England*, Vol. 4,
    1771.

SECONDARY SOURCES

General

17 Crowther, M. A., *The Workhouse System:The History of an English Social Institution*, Methuen, 1981.
18 Digby, A., *The Poor Law in Nineteenth Century England and Wales*, Historical Association, 1982.
19 Fraser, D., *The Evolution of the British Welfare State*, 2nd edn., Macmillan, 1984.
20 Novak, T., *Poverty and the State: An Historical Sociology*, Open University Press, 1988.
21 Rose, M. E., *The Relief of Poverty, 1834–1914*, 2nd edn, Macmillan, 1988.
22 Thane, P., *The Foundation of the Welfare State*, Longman, 1982.
23 Treble, J. H., *Urban Poverty in Britain, 1830–1914*, Batsford, 1979.
24 Webb, S. and B., *English Poor Law Policy*, Longman, 1910.
25 Webb, S. and B., *English Poor Law History*, Part II *The Last Hundred Years*, Longman, 1929.
26 Wood, P., *Poverty and the Workhouse in Victorian Britain*, Alan Sutton, Stroud, 1991.

Context: The Old Poor Law

27 Marshall, J. D., *The Old Poor Law*, Macmillan, 1968.
28 Dunkley, P., *The Crisis of the Old Poor Law in England, 1795–1834*, Garland, New York, 1982.
29 Oxley, G.W., *Poor Relief in England and Wales, 1601–1834*, David & Charles, Newton Abbot, 1974.
30 Poynter, F., *Society and Pauperism: English Ideas on Poor Relief, 1795–1834*, Routledge & Kegan Paul, 1969.
31 Slack, P., *The English Poor Law, 1531–1782*, Macmillan, 1991.
32 Snell, K., *Annals of the Labouring Poor: Social Change and Agrarian England, 1600–1900*, Cambridge University Press, 1988.
33 Webb, S. and B., *English Poor Law History*, Part I *The Old Poor Law*, Longman, 1927.

Economic Aspects Of The Poor Law

34 Baugh, D. A., 'The cost of poor relief in South-East England, 1780–1834', *Economic History Review*, 28, 1975.
35 Boyer, G.R., *An Economic History of the English Poor Law, 1750–1850*, Cambridge University Press, 1990.
36 Blaug, M., 'The myth of the Old Poor Law and the making of the New', *Journal of Economic History*, 23, 1963.
37 Blaug, M., 'The Poor Law report re-examined', *Journal of Economic History*, 24, 1964.
38 Caplan, M., 'The New Poor Law and the struggle for union chargeability', *International Review of Social History*, 23, 1978.

39   Coates, A.W., 'Changing attitudes to labour in the mid-eighteenth century', *Economic History Review*, 2nd ser. 11, 1958–59.

40   Coates, A.W., 'Economic thought and Poor Law policy in the eighteenth century', *Economic History Review*, 2nd ser. 13, 1960–61.

41   Coates, A.W., 'The relief of poverty: Attitudes to labour and economic change in England 1660–1782', *International Review of Social History*, 21, 1976.

42   Cowherd, R., *Political Economists and the English Poor Laws*, Ohio University Press, Athens, 1977.

43   Digby, A., 'The labour market and the continuity of social policy after 1834: the case of the eastern counties, *Economic History Review*, 2nd ser. 28, 1975.

44   Huzel, J. P., 'Malthus, the Poor Law and population in early nineteenth-century England', *Economic History Review*, 2nd ser. 22, 1969.

45   Huzel, J. P., 'The demographic impact of the Old Poor Law: More reflections on Malthus', *Economic History Review*, 2nd ser. 33, 1980.

46   Levy, S. Leon, *Nassau Senior*, Newton Abbot, David and Charles, 1970.

47   MacKinnon, M., 'Poor Law policy, unemployment and pauperism', *Explorations in Economic History*, 23, 1986.

48   MacKinnon, M., 'English Poor Law policy and the crusade against out-relief', *Journal of Economic History*, 47, 1987.

49   McCloskey, D., 'New perspectives on the Old Poor Law', *Explorations in Economic History*, 10, 1973.

50   Rose, M.E., 'The crisis of poor relief in England, 1860–1914', in W.J. Mommsen (ed.), *The Emergence of the Welfare State in Britain and Germany*, Macmillan, 1981.

51   Solar, P.M., 'Poor relief and English economic development before the industrial revolution', *Economic History Review*, 48, 1995.

Local And Regional Studies

52   Apfel, W. and Dunkley, P., 'English rural society and the New Poor Law: Bedfordshire, 1934–47', *Social History*, 10, 1985.

53   Ashforth, D., 'Settlement and removal in urban areas: Bradford, 1834–71', in M.E. Rose (ed.), *The Poor and the City*, Leicester University Press, 1985.

54   Ashforth, D., 'The treatment of poverty', in D. G. Wright and J. A. Jowitt (eds), *Victorian Bradford*, Bradford, City of Bradford Metropolitan Council, Libraries Division, 1982.

55   Boot, H.M., 'Unemployment and Poor Law relief in Manchester, 1845–59', *Social History*, 15, 1990.

56   Boyson, R., 'The New Poor Law in north east Lancashire, 1834–71', *Transactions, Lancashire and Cheshire Antiquarian Society*, 70, 1960.

57   Brundage, A., *The Making of the New Poor Law, 1832–1839*, Hutchinson, 1978.

58 Digby, A., *Pauper Palaces*, Routledge, 1978.
59 Dunkley, P., 'The hungry forties and the New Poor Law: A case study', *Historical Journal*, 2, 1974.
60 Fraser, D., 'Poor Law politics in Leeds', *Publications of the Thoresby Society*, 53, 1970.
61 Green, D.R., *From Artisans to Paupers, Economic Change and Poverty in London 1790–1870*, Scolar Press, 1995.
62 Hastings, R.P., *Poverty and the Poor Law in the North Riding of Yorkshire, 1780–1837*, University of York, Borthwick Institute for Historical Research, 1982.
63 Jones, G. S., *Outcast London: A Study in the Relationship between Classes in Victorian Society*, Oxford University Press, 1971.
64 McCord, N., 'The 1834 Poor Law Amendment Act on Tyneside', *International Review of Social History*, 14, 1969.
65 Midwinter, E. C., *Social Administration in Lancashire, 1830–1860*, Manchester University Press, 1969.
66 Rose, M.E., 'The anti Poor Law movement in the north of England', *Northern History*, I, 1966.
67 Rose, M.E., 'The New Poor Law in an industrial area', in R. Hartwell (ed.), *The Industrial Revolution*, Oxford University Press, 1970.
68 Rose, M. E. (ed.), *The Poor and the City: The English Poor Law in its Urban Context*, Leicester University Press, 1985.
69 Ryan, P., 'Politics and relief: East London unions in the late nineteenth and early twentieth centuries', in M. E. Rose (ed.), *The Poor and the City: The English Poor Law in its Urban Context*, Leicester University Press, 1985.
70 Thompson, R., 'The working of the Poor Law Amendment Act in Cumbria, 1836–1871', *Northern History*, 15, 1979.
71 Wells, R., 'Resistance to the New Poor Law in the rural south', *Middlesborogh Centre Occasional Paper* I, 1985.
72 White, G. (ed.), *In and Out of the Workhouse: The Coming of the New Poor Law to Cambridgeshire and Huntingdonshire*, Ely, 1978.
73 Williams, D., *The Rebecca Riots; A Study in Agrarian Discontent*, Cardiff, University of Wales Press, 1955.
74 Wood, P., 'Finance and the urban Poor Law: Sunderland Union, 1835–1914', in M.E. Rose (ed.), *The Poor and the City: The English Poor Law in its Urban Context*, Leicester University Press, 1985.

The Poor Law In Scotland

75 Blackden, S., 'The Poor Law and health: A survey of parochial medical aid in Glasgow, 1845–1900', in T. C. Smout (ed.), *The Search for Wealth and Stability*, Macmillan, 1979.
76 Brown, S., *Thomas Chalmers and the Godly Commonwealth in Scotland*, Oxford University Press, 1982.
77 Cage, R.A., *The Scottish Poor Law, 1745–1845*, Scottish Academic Press, Edinburgh, 1981.

78   Levitt, I., *Poverty and Welfare in Scotland 1890–1948*, John Donald, Edinburgh, 1988.

79   Levitt, I., 'The Scottish Poor Law and unemployment, 1890–1929', in T. C. Smout (ed.), *The Search for Wealth and Stability*, Macmillan, 1979.

80   Lindsay, J., *The Scottish Poor Law, Its Operation in the North East from 1745 to 1845*, Arthur H. Stockwell, Ilfracombe, 1975.

81   Mitchison, R., 'The making of the Old Scottish Poor Law', *Past & Present*, 63, 1974.

82   Mitchison, R., 'The creation of the disablement rule in the Scottish Poor Law', in T. C. Smout (ed.), *The Search for Wealth and Stability* Macmillan, 1979.

83   Mitchison, R., 'North and South: The development of the gulf in Poor Law practice', in R.A. Houston and R.D. White (eds), *Scottish Society, 1500–1800*, Cambridge University Press, 1989.

84   Mitchison, R., 'The Poor Law', in T. Devine and R. Mitchison (eds), *People, and Society in Scotland*, Vol. I, John Donald, Edinburgh, 1981.

85   Patterson, A., 'The Poor Law in nineteenth-century Scotland', in D. Fraser (ed.), *The New Poor Law in the Nineteenth Century*, Macmillan, 1976.

Social Aspects Of Poor Law Provision

86   Ayers, G.M., *England's First State Hospitals and the Metropolitan Asylums Board*, University of California Press, Berkeley and Los Angeles, 1971.

87   Bock, G. and Thane, P. (eds), *Maternity and Gender Politics: Women and the Rise of the European Welfare States, 1880s–1950s*, Routledge, 1991.

87a   Crompton, F., *Workhouse Children*, Alan Sutton, Stroud, 1997.

88   Duke, F., 'Pauper education', in D. Fraser (ed.), *The New Poor Law in the Nineteenth Century*, Macmillan, 1976.

89   Flinn, M.W., 'Medical services under the New Poor Law', in D. Fraser (ed.), *The New Poor Law in the Nineteenth Century*, Macmillan, 1976.

90   Hodgkinson, R., *The Origins of the National Health Service: The Medical Services of the New Poor Law, 1834–1871*, Wellcome, 1967.

91   Horne, P., 'Pauper apprenticeship and the Grimsby fishing industry 1870 to 1894', *Labour History Review*, 61, 1996.

92   Macdonald, H. J., 'Boarding-out and the Scottish Poor Law, 1845–1914', *Scottish Historical Review*, 75, 1996.

93   O'Neill, J. E., 'Finding a policy for the sick poor', *Victorian Studies*, 7, 1963–64.

94   Pennock, P., 'The evolution of St James's, Leeds Moral and Industrial Training School, Leeds Union Workhouse and Leeds Union Infirmary', *Publications of the Thoresby Society*, 59, 1987.

95 Thane, P., 'Women and the Poor Law in Victorian and Edwardian England', *History Workshop Journal*, 6, 1978.

96 Thomson, D., 'Falling state support for the elderly since early Victorian times', *Ageing & Society*, 4, 1984.

97 Thomson, D., 'Welfare and the historians', in L. Bonfield, R. Smith and K. Wrighton (eds), *The World We Have Gained*, Blackwell, Oxford, 1986.

OTHER SECONDARY SOURCES

 98 Ashford, W. E., *The Emergence of the Welfare States*, Blackwell, Oxford, 1986

 99 Ashforth, D., 'The urban Poor Law', in D. Fraser (ed.), *The New Poor Law in the Nineteenth Century*, Macmillan, 1976.

100 Brundage, A., 'The landed interest and the New Poor Law', *English Historical Review*, 87, 1972.

101 Brundage, A., 'The English Poor Law and the cohesion of agricultural society', *Agricultural History*, 47 1974.

102 Brundage, A. *et. al*, 'Debate: The making of the New Poor Law Redivivus', *Past and Present*, 127, 1990.

103 Burrow, J. W., *Evolution and Society, A Study in Victorian Social Theory*, Cambridge University Press, 1966.

104 Digby, A., 'The rural Poor Law', in D. Fraser (ed.), *The New Poor Law in the Nineteenth Century*, Macmillan, 1976.

105 Dandeker, C., *Surveillance, Power and Modernity: Bureaucracy and Discipline from 1700 to the Present Day*, Cambridge University Press, 1990.

106 Dickens, A., 'The architect and the workhouse', *Architectural Review*, 160, 1976.

107 Donajgrodzki, A.P. (ed.), *Social Control in Nineteenth Century Britain*, Croom Helm, 1977.

108 Driver, F., *Power and Pauperism: The Workhouse System, 1834–1884*, Cambridge University Press, 1993.

109 Dunkley, P., 'The landed interest and the making of the New Poor Law: a critical note', *English Historical Review*, 88, 1973.

110 Dunkley, P., 'Whigs and paupers: The reform of the English Poor Law, 1830–34', *Journal of British Studies*, 20, 1981.

111 Edsall, N. C., *The Anti Poor Law Movement, 1834–1844*, Manchester University Press, 1971.

112 Englander, D., *Landlord and Tenant in Urban Britain, 1838–1918*, Clarendon Press, Oxford, 1983.

113 Englander, D. and O'Day, R. (eds), *Retrieved Riches: Social Investigation in Britain 1840–1914*, Scolar Press, 1995.

114 Englander, D., 'Comparisons and contrasts: Henry Mayhew and Charles Booth as social investigators', in David Englander and

Rosemary O'Day, (eds), *Retrieved Riches: Social Investigation in Britain 1840–1914*, Scolar Press, 1995.

115 Finer, S.E., *The Life and Times of Sir Edwin Chadwick*, Methuen, 1952.

116 Fraser, D., 'The Poor Law as a political institution', in D. Fraser (ed.), *The New Poor Law in the Nineteenth Century*, Macmillan, 1975.

117 Fraser, D., 'The English Poor Law and the origins of the British welfare state' in W. J. Mommsen (ed.), *The Emergence of the Welfare State in Britain and Germany, 1850–1914*, Macmillan, 1981.

118 Gillie, A., 'The origin of the poverty line', *Economic History Review*, 49, 1996.

119 Harris, J., *Unemployment and British Politics, 1886–1914*, Oxford University Press, 1972.

120 Harris, J., 'Between civic virtue and Social Darwinism: The concept of the residuum', in David Englander and Rosemary O'Day (eds), *Retrieved Riches: Social Investigation in Britain 1840–1914*, Scolar Press, 1995.

121 Hart, J., 'Nineteenth-century social reform: a Tory interpretation of history', *Past and Present*, 31, 1965.

122 Hennock, E.P., 'Poverty and social theory in England: the experience of the eighteen-eighties', *Social History*, 1, 1976.

123 Henriques, U., 'How cruel was the Victorian Poor Law?', *Historical Journal*, 11, 1968.

124 Himmelfarb, G., *The Idea of Poverty, England in the Early Industrial Age*, Faber, 1984.

125 Himmelfarb, G., *Poverty and Compassion: The Moral Imagination of the Late Victorians*, Knopf, New York, 1991.

126 Hume, L. J., *Bentham and Bureaucracy*, Cambridge University Press, 1981.

127 Humphery, R., *Sin, Organised Charity and the Poor Law in Victorian England*, St Martin's Press, 1995.

128 Jones, G. S., *Languages of Class*, Cambridge University Press, 1983.

129 Keating, P. J., *The Working Class in Victorian Fiction*, Routledge, 1971.

130 Kidd, A.J., 'Historians or polemicists? How the Webbs wrote their history of the English Poor Laws', *Economic History Review*, 40, 1987.

131 Lees, L., 'The Survival of the unfit: Welfare policies and family maintenance in nineteenth-century London' in P. Mandler (ed.), *The Uses of Charity: The Poor on Relief in the Nineteenth-Century Metropolis*, University of Pennsylvania Press, Philadelphia, 1990.

132 Lewis, J., *Women and Social Action in Victorian and Edwardian England*, Edward Elgar, 1993.

133 Lewis, J., *The Voluntary Sector, the State and Social Work in Britain: The Charity Organization Society*, Edward Elgar, 1995.

134 Longmate, N., *The Workhouse*, Temple-Smith, 1974.
135 Macdonagh, O., 'The nineteenth-century revolution in government: A reappraisal', *Historical Journal*, 1, 1958.
136 McBriar, A. M., *An Edwardian Mixed Doubles, The Bosanquets versus the Webbs, A Study in British Social Policy, 1890–1929* Clarendon Press, Oxford, 1987.
137 McBriar, A. M., 'Charles Booth and the Royal Commission on the Poor Laws, 1905–9'; *Historical Studies*, [Melbourne] 51, 1973.
138 McCord, N., 'The Poor Law and philanthropy', in D. Fraser (ed.), *The New Poor Law in the Nineteenth Century*, Macmillan, 1976.
139 McCord, N., 'Ratepayers and social policy', in P. Thane (ed.), *The Origins of British Social Policy*, Croom Helm, 1978.
140 Mandler, P., 'The making of the New Poor Law *Redivivus*', *Past and Present*, 117, 1987.
141 Marshall, A., 'The Poor Law in relation to state-aided pensions', *Economic Journal*, 2, 1892.
142 Martin, E .W., 'From parish to union', in E.E. Martin (ed.), *Comparative Development in Social Welfare*, 1972.
143 O'Day, R., *The Family and Family Relationships 1500–1900*, Macmillan, 1994.
144 O'Day, R. and Englander, D., *Mr Charles Booth's Inquiry, Life and Labour of the People in London Reconsidered*, Hambledon Press, 1993.
145 O'Day, R., 'Women and social investigation: Clara Collet and Beatrice Potter' in David Englander and Rosemary O'Day (eds.), *Retrieved Riches: Social Investigation in Britain 1840–1914*, Scolar Press, 1995.
146 O'Day, R., *Katharine Buildings, East Smithfield, 1880–1914*, forthcoming.
147 Parris, H., 'The nineteenth-century revolution in government: A reappraisal reappraised', *Historical Journal*, 3, 1960.
148 Perkin, H., 'Individualism versus collectivism in nineteenth-century Britain: A false antithesis', *Journal of British Studies*, 17, 1977.
149 Pollard, S., 'Labour in Great Britain' in S. Pollard (ed.), *The Cambridge Economic History of Europe: The Industrial Economies*, Part I, VII, Cambridge University Press, 1978.
150 Prest, J., *Liberty and Locality: Parliament, Permissive Legislation and Ratepayers' Democracies in the Nineteenth Century*, Oxford University Press, 1990.
151 Roberts, D., *Victorian Origins of the Welfare State*, Yale University Press, New Haven, 1960.
152 Roberts, D., 'How cruel was the Victorian Poor Law?', *Historical Journal*, 4, 1963.
153 Rose, M.E., 'The allowance system under the New Poor Law', *Economic History Review*, 2nd ser., 19, 1966.
154 Rose, M. E., 'The anti-poor law agitation', in J. T. Ward (ed.), *Popular Movements, 1830–1850*, Batsford, 1970.

155 Rose, M.E., 'Settlement removal and the New Poor Law' in D. Fraser (ed.), *The New Poor Law in the Nineteenth Century*, Macmillan, 1976.

156 Tawney, R.H., *Religion and the Rise of Capitalism*, Penguin, Harmondsworth, 1938.

157 Thompson, E.P., *The Making of the English Working Class*, Vintage Books, New York, 1963.

158 Thompson, F. M. L., 'Social control in Victorian Britain', *Economic History Review*, 2nd ser., 34, 1981.

159 Veit-Wilson, J. H., 'Paradigms of poverty: A rehabilitation of B. S. Rowntree' in David Englander and Rosemary O'Day (eds), *Retrieved Riches: Social investigation in Britain 1840–1914*, Scolar Press, 1995.

160 Vincent, A., and Plant, R., *Philosophy, Politics and Citizenship, The Life and Thought of the British Idealists*, Blackwell, Oxford, 1984.

161 Vorspan, R., 'Vagrancy and the New Poor Law in late Victorian and Edwardian England', *English Historical Review*, 92, 1977.

162 Weaver, S.A., *John Fielden and the Politics of Popular Radicalism, 1832–1847*, Oxford University Press, 1987.

163 Williams, K., *From Pauperism to Poverty*, Routledge & Kegan Paul, 1978.

164 Woodroofe, K., 'The Royal Commission on the Poor Laws, 1905–9', *International Review of Social History*, 22, 1977.

165 Yeo, E., *The Contest for Social Science: Relations and Representations of Gender and Class*, Rivers Oram Press, 1996.

INDEX